New Technologies and Reference Services

New Technologies and Reference Services has been co-published simultaneously as *The Reference Librarian*, Number 71 2000.

The *Reference Librarian* Monographic "Separates"

Below is a list of "separates," which in serials librarianship means a special issue simultaneously published as a special journal issue or double-issue *and* as a "separate" hardbound monograph. (This is a format which we also call a "DocuSerial.")

"Separates" are published because specialized libraries or professionals may wish to purchase a specific thematic issue by itself in a format which can be separately cataloged and shelved, as opposed to purchasing the journal on an on-going basis. Faculty members may also more easily consider a "separate" for classroom adoption.

"Separates" are carefully classified separately with the major book jobbers so that the journal tie-in can be noted on new book order slips to avoid duplicate purchasing.

You may wish to visit Haworth's website at . . .

http://www.HaworthPress.com

. . . to search our online catalog for complete tables of contents of these separates and related publications.

You may also call 1-800-HAWORTH (outside US/Canada: 607-722-5857), or Fax 1-800-895-0582 (outside US/Canada: 607-771-0012), or e-mail at:

getinfo@haworthpressinc.com

New Technologies and Reference Services, edited by Bill Katz, PhD (No. 71, 2000). *This important book explores developing trends in publishing, information literacy in the reference environment, reference provision in adult basic and community education, searching sessions, outreach programs, locating moving image materials for multimedia development, and much more.*

Reference Services for the Adult Learner: Challenging Issues for the Traditional and Technological Era, edited by Kwasi Sarkodie-Mensah, PhD (No. 69/70, 2000). *Containing research from librarians and adult learners from the United States, Canada, and Australia, this comprehensive guide offers you strategies for teaching adult patrons that will enable them to properly use and easily locate all of the materials in your library.*

Library Outreach, Partnerships, and Distance Education: Reference Librarians at the Gateway, edited by Wendi Arant and Pixey Anne Mosley (No. 67/68, 1999). *Focuses on community outreach in libraries toward a broader public by extending services based on recent developments in information technology.*

From Past-Present to Future-Perfect: A Tribute to Charles A. Bunge and the Challenges of Contemporary Reference Service, edited by Chris D. Ferguson, PhD (No. 66, 1999). *Explore reprints of selected articles by Charles Bunge, bibliographies of his published work, and original articles that draw on Bunge's values and ideas in assessing the present and shaping the future of reference service.*

Reference Services and Media, edited by Martha Merrill, PhD (No. 65, 1999). *Gives you valuable information about various aspects of reference services and media, including changes, planning issues, and the use and impact of new technologies.*

Coming of Age in Reference Services: A Case History of the Washington State University Libraries, edited by Christy Zlatos, MSLS (No. 64, 1999). *A celebration of the perserverance, ingenuity, and talent of the librarians who have served, past and present, at the Holland Library reference desk.*

Document Delivery Services: Contrasting Views, edited by Robin Kinder, MLS (No. 63, 1999). *Reviews the planning and process of implementing document delivery in four university libraries–Miami University, University of Colorado at Denver, University of Montana at Missoula, and Purdue University Libraries.*

The Holocaust: Memories, Research, Reference, edited by Robert Hauptman, PhD, and Susan Hubbs Motin (No. 61/62, 1998). *"A wonderful resource for reference librarians, students, and teachers . . . on how to present this painful, historical event." (Ephraim Kaye, PhD, The International School for Holocaust Studies, Yad Vashem, Jerusalem)*

Electronic Resources: Use and User Behavior, edited by Hemalata Iyer, PhD (No. 60, 1998). *Covers electronic resources and their use in libraries, with emphasis on the Internet and the Geographic Information Systems (GIS).*

Philosophies of Reference Service, edited by Celia Hales Mabry (No. 59, 1997). *"Recommended reading for any manager responsible for managing reference services and hiring reference librarians in any type of library." (Charles R. Anderson, MLS, Associate Director for Public Services, King County Library System, Bellevue, Washington)*

Business Reference Services and Sources: How End Users and Librarians Work Together, edited by Katherine M. Shelfer (No. 58, 1997). *"This is an important collection of papers suitable for all business librarians. . . . Highly recommended!" (Lucy Heckman, MLS, MBA, Business and Economics Reference Librarian, St. John's University, Jamaica, New York)*

Reference Sources on the Internet: Off the Shelf and onto the Web, edited by Karen R. Diaz (No. 57, 1997). *Surf off the library shelves and onto the Internet and cut your research time in half!*

Reference Services for Archives and Manuscripts, edited by Laura B. Cohen (No. 56, 1997). *"Features stimulating and interesting essays on security in archives, ethics in the archival profession, and electronic records." ("The Year's Best Professional Reading" (1998), Library Journal)*

Career Planning and Job Searching in the Information Age, edited by Elizabeth A. Lorenzen, MLS (No. 55, 1996). *"Offers stimulating background for dealing with the issues of technology and service. . . . A reference tool to be looked at often." (The One-Person Library)*

The Roles of Reference Librarians: Today and Tomorrow, edited by Kathleen Low, MLS (No. 54, 1996). *"A great asset to all reference collections. . . . Presents important, valuable information for reference librarians as well as other library users." (Library Times International)*

Reference Services for the Unserved, edited by Fay Zipkowitz, MSLS, DA (No. 53, 1996). *"A useful tool in developing strategies to provide services to all patrons." (Science Books & Films)*

Library Instruction Revisited: Bibliographic Instruction Comes of Age, edited by Lyn Elizabeth M. Martin, MLS (No. 51/52, 1995). *"A powerful collection authored by respected practitioners who have stormed the bibliographic instruction (BI) trenches and, luckily for us, have recounted their successes and shortcomings." (The Journal of Academic Librarianship)*

Library Users and Reference Services, edited by Jo Bell Whitlatch, PhD (No. 49/50, 1995). *"Well-planned, balanced, and informative. . . . Both new and seasoned professionals will find material for service attitude formation and practical advice for the front lines of service." (Anna M. Donnelly, MS, MA, Associate Professor and Reference Librarian, St. John's University Library)*

Social Science Reference Services, edited by Pam Baxter, MLS (No. 48, 1995). *"Offers practical guidance to the reference librarian. . . . A valuable source of information about specific literatures within the social sciences and the skills and techniques needed to provide access to those literatures." (Nancy P. O'Brien, MLS, Head, Education and Social Science Library, and Professor of Library Administration, University of Illinois at Urbana-Champaign)*

Reference Services in the Humanities, edited by Judy Reynolds, MLS (No. 47, 1994). *"A well-chosen collection of situations and challenges encountered by reference librarians in the humanities." (College Research Library News)*

Racial and Ethnic Diversity in Academic Libraries: Multicultural Issues, edited by Deborah A. Curry, MLS, MA, Susan Griswold Blandy, MEd, and Lyn Elizabeth M. Martin, MLS

(No. 45/46, 1994). *"The useful techniques and attractive strategies presented here will provide the incentive for fellow professionals in academic libraries around the country to go and do likewise in their own institutions." (David Cohen, Adjunct Professor of Library Science, School of Library and Information Science, Queens College; Director, EMIE (Ethnic Materials Information Exchange); Editor, EMIE Bulletin)*

School Library Reference Services in the 90s: Where We Are, Where We're Heading, edited by Carol Truett, PhD (No. 44, 1994). *"Unique and valuable to the the teacher-librarian as well as students of librarianship. . . . The overall work successfully interweaves the concept of the continuously changing role of the teacher-librarian." (Emergency Librarian)*

Reference Services Planning in the 90s, edited by Gail Z. Eckwright, MLS, and Lori M. Keenan, MLS (No. 43, 1994). *"This monograph is well-researched and definitive, encompassing reference service as practices by library and information scientists. . . . It should be required reading for all professional librarian trainees." (Feliciter)*

Librarians on the Internet: Impact on Reference Services, edited by Robin Kinder, MLS (No. 41/42, 1994). *"Succeeds in demonstrating that the Internet is becoming increasingly a challenging but practical and manageable tool in the reference librarian's ever-expanding armory." (Reference Reviews)*

Reference Service Expertise, edited by Bill Katz (No. 40, 1993). *This important volume presents a wealth of practical ideas for improving the art of reference librarianship.*

Modern Library Technology and Reference Services, edited by Samuel T. Huang, MLS, MS (No. 39, 1993). *"This book packs a surprising amount of information into a relatively few number of pages. . . . This book will answer many questions." (Science Books and Films)*

Assessment and Accountability in Reference Work, edited by Susan Griswold Blandy, Lyn M. Martin, and Mary L. Strife (No. 38, 1992). *"An important collection of well-written, real-world chapters addressing the central questions that surround performance and services in all libraries." (Library Times International)*

The Reference Librarian and Implications of Mediation, edited by M. Keith Ewing, MLS, and Robert Hauptman, MLS (No. 37, 1992). *"An excellent and thorough analysis of reference mediation. . . . Well worth reading by anyone involved in the delivery of reference services." (Fred Batt, MLS, Associate University Librarian for Public Services, California State University, Sacramento)*

Library Services for Career Planning, Job Searching and Employment Opportunities, edited by Byron Anderson, MA, MLS (No. 36, 1992). *"An interesting book which tells professional libraries how to set up career information centers. . . . Clearly valuable reading for anyone establishing a career library." (Career Opportunities News)*

In the Spirit of 1992: Access to Western European Libraries and Literature, edited by Mary M. Huston, PhD, and Maureen Pastine, MLS (No. 35, 1992). *"A valuable and practical [collection] which every subject specialist in the field would do well to consult." (Western European Specialists Section Newsletter)*

Access Services: The Convergence of Reference and Technical Services, edited by Gillian M. McCombs, ALA (No. 34, 1992). *"Deserves a wide readership among both technical and public services librarians. . . . Highly recommended for any librarian interested in how reference and technical services roles may be combined." (Library Resources & Technical Services)*

Opportunities for Reference Services: The Bright Side of Reference Services in the 1990s, edited by Bill Katz (No. 33, 1991). *"A well-deserved look at the brighter side of reference services. . . . Should be read by reference librarians and their administrators in all types of libraries." (Library Times International)*

Government Documents and Reference Services, edited by Robin Kinder, MLS (No. 32, 1991). *Discusses access possibilities and policies with regard to government information, covering such important topics as new and impending legislation, information on most frequently used and requested sources, and grant writing.*

The Reference Library User: Problems and Solutions, edited by Bill Katz (No. 31, 1991).
  "Valuable information and tangible suggestions that will help us as a profession look critically at our users and decide how they are best served." (Information Technology and Libraries)

Continuing Education of Reference Librarians, edited by Bill Katz (No. 30/31, 1990). *"Has something for everyone interested in this field.... Library trainers and library school teachers may well find stimulus in some of the programs outlined here." (Library Association Record)*

Weeding and Maintenance of Reference Collections, edited by Sydney J. Pierce, PhD, MLS (No. 29, 1990). *"This volume may spur you on to planned activity before lack of space dictates 'ad hoc' solutions." (New Library World)*

Serials and Reference Services, edited by Robin Kinder, MLS, and Bill Katz (No. 27/28, 1990). *"The concerns and problems discussed are those of serials and reference librarians everywhere.... The writing is of a high standard and the book is useful and entertaining.... This book can be recommended." (Library Association Record)*

Rothstein on Reference: ... with some help from friends, edited by Bill Katz and Charles Bunge, PhD, MLS (No. 25/26, 1990). *"An important and stimulating collection of essays on reference librarianship.... Highly recommended!" (Richard W. Grefrath, MA, MLS, Reference Librarian, University of Nevada Library)* Dedicated to the work of Sam Rothstein, one of the world's most respected teachers of reference librarians, this special volume features his writings as well as articles written about him and his teachings by other professionals in the field.

Integrating Library Use Skills Into the General Education Curriculum, edited by Maureen Pastine, MLS, and Bill Katz (No. 24, 1989). *"All contributions are written and presented to a high standard with excellent references at the end of each.... One of the best summaries I have seen on this topic." (Australian Library Review)*

Expert Systems in Reference Services, edited by Christine Roysdon, MLS, and Howard D. White, PhD, MLS (No. 23, 1989). *"The single most comprehensive work on the subject of expert systems in reference service." (Information Processing and Management)*

Information Brokers and Reference Services, edited by Bill Katz and Robin Kinder, MLS (No. 22, 1989). *"An excellent tool for reference librarians and indispensable for anyone seriously considering their own information-brokering service." (Booklist)*

Information and Referral in Reference Services, edited by Marcia Stucklen Middleton, MLS and Bill Katz (No. 21, 1988). *Investigates a wide variety of situations and models which fall under the umbrella of information and referral.*

Reference Services and Public Policy, edited by Richard Irving, MLS, and Bill Katz (No. 20, 1988). *Looks at the relationship between public policy and information and reports ways in which libraries respond to the need for public policy information.*

Finance, Budget, and Management for Reference Services, edited by Ruth A. Fraley, MLS, MBA, and Bill Katz (No. 19, 1989). *"Interesting and relevant to the current state of financial needs in reference service.... A must for anyone new to or already working in the reference service area." (Riverina Library Review)*

Current Trends in Information: Research and Theory, edited by Bill Katz and Robin Kinder, MLS (No. 18, 1984). *"Practical direction to improve reference services and does so in a variety of ways ranging from humorous and clever metaphoric comparisons to systematic and practical methodological descriptions." (American Reference Books Annual)*

International Aspects of Reference and Information Services, edited by Bill Katz and Ruth A. Fraley, MLS, MBA (No. 17, 1987). *"An informative collection of essays written by eminent librarians, library school staff, and others concerned with the international aspects of information work." (Library Association Record)*

Reference Services Today: From Interview to Burnout, edited by Bill Katz and Ruth A. Fraley, MLS, MBA (No. 16, 1987). *Authorities present important advice to all reference librarians on the improvement of service and the enhancement of the public image of reference services.*

The Publishing and Review of Reference Sources, edited by Bill Katz and Robin Kinder, MLS (No. 15, 1987). *"A good review of current reference reviewing and publishing trends in the United States . . . will be of interest to intending reviewers, reference librarians, and students." (Australasian College Libraries)*

Personnel Issues in Reference Services, edited by Bill Katz and Ruth Fraley, MLS, MBA (No. 14, 1986). *"Chock-full of information that can be applied to most reference settings. Recommended for libraries with active reference departments." (RQ)*

Reference Services in Archives, edited by Lucille Whalen (No. 13, 1986). *"Valuable for the insights it provides on the reference process in archives and as a source of information on the different ways of carrying out that process." (Library and Information Science Annual)*

Conflicts in Reference Services, edited by Bill Katz and Ruth A. Fraley, MLS, MBA (No. 12, 1985). *This collection examines issues pertinent to the reference department.*

Evaluation of Reference Services, edited by Bill Katz and Ruth A. Fraley, MLS, MBA (No. 11, 1985). *"A much-needed overview of the present state of the art vis-à-vis reference service evaluation. . . . Excellent. . . . Will appeal to reference professionals and aspiring students." (RQ)*

Library Instruction and Reference Services, edited by Bill Katz and Ruth A. Fraley, MLS, MBA (No. 10, 1984). *"Well written, clear, and exciting to read. This is an important work recommended for all librarians, particularly those involved in, interested in, or considering bibliographic instruction. . . . A milestone in library literature." (RQ)*

Reference Services and Technical Services: Interactions in Library Practice, edited by Gordon Stevenson and Sally Stevenson (No. 9, 1984). *"New ideas and longstanding problems are handled with humor and sensitivity as practical suggestions and new perspectives are suggested by the authors." (Information Retrieval & Library Automation)*

Reference Services for Children and Young Adults, edited by Bill Katz and Ruth A. Fraley, MLS, MBA (No. 7/8, 1983). *"Offers a well-balanced approach to reference service for children and young adults. " (RQ)*

Video to Online: Reference Services in the New Technology, edited by Bill Katz and Ruth A. Fraley, MLS, MBA (No. 5/6, 1983). *"A good reference manual to have on hand. . . . Well-written, concise, provide[s] a wealth of information." (Online)*

Ethics and Reference Services, edited by Bill Katz and Ruth A. Fraley, MLS, MBA (No. 4, 1982). *Library experts discuss the major ethical and legal implications that reference librarians must take into consideration when handling sensitive inquiries about confidential material.*

Reference Services Administration and Management, edited by Bill Katz and Ruth A. Fraley, MLS, MBA (No. 3, 1982). *Librarianship experts discuss the management of the reference function in libraries and information centers, outlining the responsibilities and qualifications of reference heads.*

Reference Services in the 1980s, edited by Bill Katz (No. 1/2, 1982). *Here is a thought-provoking volume on the future of reference services in libraries, with an emphasis on the challenges and needs that have come about as a result of automation.*

New Technologies and Reference Services

Bill Katz
Editor

New Technologies and Reference Services has been co-published simultaneously as *The Reference Librarian*, Number 71 2000.

The Haworth Information Press
An Imprint of
The Haworth Press, Inc.
New York • London • Oxford

Published by

The Haworth Press Information Press, 10 Alice Street, Binghamton, NY 13904-1580, USA

The Haworth Information Press, is an imprint of The Haworth Press, Inc., 10 Alice Street, Binghamton, NY 13904-1580 USA

New Technologies and Reference Services has been co-published simultaneously as *The Reference Librarian*, Number 71 2000.

The development, preparation, and publication of this work has been undertaken with great care. However, the publisher, employees, editors, and agents of The Haworth Press and all imprints of The Haworth Press, Inc., including The Haworth Medical Press® and Pharmaceutical Products Press®, are not responsible for any errors contained herein or for consequences that may ensue from use of materials or information contained in this work. Opinions expressed by the author(s) are not necessarily those of The Haworth Press, Inc.

Cover design by Thomas J. Mayshock Jr.

Library of Congress Cataloging-in-Publication Data

New technologies and reference services/Bill Katz, editor.
     p. cm.
     "Co-published simultaneously as The reference librarian, number 71, 2000."
     Includes bibliographical references and index.
     ISBN 0-7890-1180 (acid-free paper–ISBN 0-7890-1181-6 (pbk.: acid-free paper)
     1. Reference services (Libraries)–United States. 2. Multimedia library services–United States. 3. Academic libraries–Reference services–United States. 4. Electronic reference services (Libraries–United States. 5. Libraries–United States–Special collections–Electronic reference sources. I. Katz, William A., 1924-

Z711 .N46 2000
025.5′2–dc21

00-057555

Indexing, Abstracting & Website/Internet Coverage

This section provides you with a list of major indexing & abstracting services. That is to say, each service began covering this periodical during the year noted in the right column. Most Websites which are listed below have indicated that they will either post, disseminate, compile, archive, cite or alert their own Website users with research-based content from this work. (This list is as current as the copyright date of this publication.)

Abstracting, Website/Indexing Coverage .... Year When Coverage Began

- *Academic Abstracts/CD-ROM* **1995**
- *Academic Search: data base of 2,000 selected academic serials, updated monthly: EBSCO Publishing* **1996**
- *BUBL Information Service: An Internet-Based Information Service for the UK Higher Education Community <URL:http://bubl.ac.uk/>* **1994**
- *CNPIEC Reference Guide: Chinese National Directory of Foreign Periodicals* **1996**
- *Current Awareness Abstracts of Library & Information Literature, ASLIB (UK)* **1992**
- *Current Index to Journals in Education* **1992**
- *Educational Administration Abstracts (EAA)* **1992**
- *FINDEX <www.publist.com>* **1999**
- *Handbook of Latin American Studies* **1999**
- *IBZ International Bibliography of Periodical Literature* **1995**
- *Index to Periodical Articles Related to Law* **1992**
- *Information Science Abstracts* **1992**
- *Informed Librarian, The <http://www.infosourcespub.com>* **1993**

(continued)

Special bibliographic notes related to special journal issues (separates) and indexing/abstracting:

- indexing/abstracting services in this list will also cover material in any "separate" that is co-published simultaneously with Haworth's special thematic journal issue or DocuSerial. Indexing/abstracting usually covers material at the article/chapter level.
- monographic co-editions are intended for either non-subscribers or libraries which intend to purchase a second copy for their circulating collections.
- monographic co-editions are reported to all jobbers/wholesalers/approval plans. The source journal is listed as the "series" to assist the prevention of duplicate purchasing in the same manner utilized for books-in-series.
- to facilitate user/access services all indexing/abstracting services are encouraged to utilize the co-indexing entry note indicated at the bottom of the first page of each article/chapter/contribution.
- this is intended to assist a library user of any reference tool (whether print, electronic, online, or CD-ROM) to locate the monographic version if the library has purchased this version but not a subscription to the source journal.
- individual articles/chapters in any Haworth publication are also available through the Haworth Document Delivery Service (HDDS).

New Technologies and Reference Services

CONTENTS

SELECTION FOR USERS

SERVICE FOR WHOM?

ABOUT THE EDITOR

Bill Katz is Editor of *The Reference Librarian* and *The Acquisitions Librarian* and Professor Emeritus of Information Science, SUNY, Albany, New York.

Introduction

Bill Katz

Not too many years ago a reference librarian mastered a few reference books, picked-up the skills of the reference interview and how not to insult someone on the telephone when a long line of eager readers was in front of the desk. Aside from a cursory knowledge of interlibrary loan and matters related to book selection, budgets and vacations there was not too much more to know.

Those, truly, were the good old days.

Interference in this halcyon world arrived with the computer. Things will never be the same again. True, it is now much easier, more efficient and even more rewarding to pick data out of the atmosphere rather than from a book. True, there are thousands, if not millions of more choices. Unfortunately, the other truth is that to take advantage of these developing information channels one must not only learn the delights of a VCR, but the workings of networks, search engines, chat groups and the ubiquitous Web. Throw in a three day course on mechanics, changing paper and ink sources on a printer and the byways of what to do when the PC shuts down and the average librarian often is ready to go back to filling paste pots.

Somewhere in the middle of the new, the old and the reference work place is the ubiquitous user, patron, reader or traveller down the information highway. (There never has been a totally rewarding descriptor for the individual who wants help from a reference librarian.) The question today no longer is one of overcoming the drawbacks of the

Bill Katz is Editor of *The Reference Librarian* and *The Acquisitions Librarian* and Professor Emeritus, School of Information Science, SUNY, Albany, New York.

[Haworth co-indexing entry note]: "Introduction." Katz, Bill. Co-published simultaneously in *The Reference Librarian* (The Haworth Information Press, an imprint of The Haworth Press, Inc.) No. 71, 2000, pp. 1-2; and: *New Technologies and Reference Services* (ed: Bill Katz) The Haworth Information Press, an imprint of The Haworth Press, Inc., 2000, pp. 1-2. Single or multiple copies of this article are available for a fee from The Haworth Document Delivery Service [1-800-342-9678, 9:00 a.m. - 5:00 p.m. (EST). E-mail address: getinfo@haworthpressinc.com].

1

new technologies, but how to use them to make the individual who is seeking information satisfied with the answers those technologies call up.

Here the focus in on diversity, on a general overall view of how to use a computer to help someone find the meaning of life to how to acquaint adults, students and all with what the library can offer them via the new approaches to data.

The future of reference services is much more than the future of the computer. It is the future of people such as yourself who have the imagination and curiosity to harness technology to help readers. And that's what this volume is all about.

WELCOME TO THE MILLENNIUM

In the Blink of an Eye:
Developing Trends in Publishing

Jeanne W. Merrill

SUMMARY. The publishing business has become a quickly changing kaleidoscope of new ideas as well as a creative reworking of old concepts. The death of the book has been predicted for countless years. This paper will examine some broad trends in publishing during the past few years and what they mean for the publishing business; libraries and librarians; the various formats of print, CD-ROM, and online; archiving; copyright; and for the technological "have-nots" in the future. The development of K-12 resources, branding, and value-added services are also discussed. It will explore the offerings of selected publishers including The Thompson Corporation, Bell & Howell Information and Learning, Facts On File, and netLibrary in order to see, what, if

Jeanne W. Merrill is a Trained Classicist who is now Head of the Geier Library at Berkshire School, an independent, secondary school for boarding and day students, grades nine through twelve.

Address correspondence to: Jeanne W. Merrill, Geier Library, Berkshire School, 245 North Undermountain Road, Sheffield, MA 01257 (E-mail: tully63@bcn.net).

[Haworth co-indexing entry note]: "In the Blink of an Eye: Developing Trends in Publishing." Merrill, Jeanne W. Co-published simultaneously in *The Reference Librarian* (The Haworth Information Press, an imprint of The Haworth Press, Inc.) No. 71, 2000, pp. 3-24; and: *New Technologies and Reference Services* (ed: Bill Katz) The Haworth Information Press, an imprint of The Haworth Press, Inc., 2000, pp. 3-24. Single or multiple copies of this article are available for a fee from The Haworth Document Delivery Service [1-800-342-9678, 9:00 a.m. - 5:00 p.m. (EST). E-mail address: getinfo@haworthpressinc.com].

any, trends can be established. *[Article copies available for a fee from The Haworth Document Delivery Service: 1-800-342-9678. E-mail address: <getinfo@ haworthpressinc.com> Website: <http://www.HaworthPress.com>]*

KEYWORDS. Publishers and publishing, K-12 resources, copyright, reference service trends

There is nothing in this world constant, but inconstancy.

–Jonathan Swift. *The Drapier's Letters*, No. 2 (4 Aug. 1724)

The publishing business has become a quickly changing kaleidoscope of new ideas as well as a creative reworking of old concepts. The death of the book has been predicted for countless years. Publishers of reference resources and librarians are changing the way research is and will be done as well the role of the librarian in the process. This paper will examine some broad trends in publishing during the past few years and what they mean for the publishing business; libraries and librarians; the various formats of print, CD-ROM, and online; archiving; copyright; and for the technological "have-nots" in the future. The offerings of selected publishers of reference resources will also be examined in order to see what trends, if any, can be determined.

In less than fifteen years, technological developments of the Internet and the World Wide Web have dramatically changed the way publishers operate as well as the way in which they are structured. In 1986, the world's first free, public Internet access was established. Tim Berners-Lee first proposed the World Wide Web while he was working for CERN (Centre Européan pour la Reserche Nucléaire–European Laboratory for Particle Physics) in Geneva, Switzerland. By 1991, his hypertext-based software was completed. Mosaic, the first point-and click browser with a graphical user interface (GUI), was developed in 1993; and Yahoo!, a controlled, hierarchical subject-based Web directory, came along just one year later in 1994. In 1995, Java, a platform-independent programming language which can run on any graphical user interface-based system, was introduced. Java and Java applets have greatly increased the speed with which items, especially those of a graphical nature, can be retrieved. By 1998, XML (Extensible Markup Language), a simplified version of HTML, allowed authors to use XML tabs which contain information about the content of the text as well as how that information is to be displayed.[1] These advances have allowed many publishers to broaden their market share and exposure because of the increased ease of engaging in e-commerce.

In the late summer of 1999, two events happened which are significant in the history of book publishing. *Knockdown: The Harrowing Account of a Yacht Race That Turned Bad* by Martin Dugard made history. A title, which at the time was expected to be commercially successful, appeared in an electronic version six weeks before its August 30th hardcover release date. *Knockdown* was available for download in Softbook and Rocket eBook editions as well as in a print-on-demand version–so much for the paperless society–from Replica Books, Sprout, Inc., and Lightning Print, Inc. The print-on-demand version was withdrawn as soon as the hardcover edition was released. All three versions sold for the same price.[2] Whether or not the e-book with its hypertext capabilities will become the replacement for reference and technical books as well as the paperback of the average consumer remains to be seen. Problems with data permanence, display capabilities, durability, and copying are still much in evidence.[3] About the same time James Strachan, the European head of Britannica, founded in 1768, announced that "The economics of the encyclopedia business mean that it is far more profitable . . . to concentrate on electronic publishing rather than book publishing."[4]

ENCYCLOPEDIAS

The market for online encyclopedias has grown with incredible speed. *Grolier's American Encyclopedia,* the first encyclopedia on CD-ROM, was offered in 1985, and Compton's introduced the first multimedia encyclopedia in 1989. Late in 1994, *Encyclopedia Britannica* became the first Internet encyclopedia. By 1999 it appeared likely that the current print version of *Britannica* would be the last. In October 1999 *Encyclopedia Britannica* announced that it was offering its encyclopedia free to Americans on the Internet at *http://www.britannica. com.* This move may change the publishing of encyclopedias, their format, quality, and content forever. This is a good example of one of the new and creative ways publishers are doing e-commerce on the Internet. Britannica's partners in this venture include Excalibur, a high-performance retrieval specialist, Merriam-Webster, the Washington Post, Newsweek, and Barnes & Noble. The encyclopedia is also supported by advertising. The site includes the complete, updated *Britannica*, articles from more than seventy periodicals like *Newsweek* and *The Economist*, and current events from *http://www.washingtonpost.com*. It also includes a guide to over 125,000 of the Web's best sites. A search of the encyclopedia will give the user four columns that have information specifically about the topic searched or mention the topic in passing: encyclopedia articles, the Web's best sites, magazines, and related books. Essentially, the *Encyclopedia Britannica* and *Merriam-Webster's Collegiate Dictionary*, capitalizing on brand name recognition, are being offered free in order to attract customers to Britannica's sponsors and to Britannica.com's online store where books, CD-ROMs, and scientific kits and equipment can be purchased. Print offerings include the 1999 print version of *Britannica* along with CD and *Yearbook* ($1,250.00), *Britannica First Edition Replica* set ($195.00), and *Merriam-Webster's Encyclopedia of World Religions* ($34.95). Various editions of *Britannica* on CD-ROM are offered, including the *Britannica CD 2000 Deluxe* ($69.00 with various discounts applicable). The alliance of respected publishers of reference materials with more commercial companies is a growing trend in publishing. It remains to be seen whether the quality and content will remain first rate in the future.

Such elimination of print versions of encyclopedias is a growing trend. In 1997, William Katz listed seven major multi-volume, general encyclopedias.[5] By the *Encyclopedia Update, 1999* in the *Reference Books Bulletin*, just two years later, there are only four general, multi-volume encyclopedias available in print–two of which are from the same publisher. ". . . it has become apparent that if we continued to devote the September Update to print versions we'd soon have nothing to talk about. The only encyclopedias available as printed books this year are *Encyclopedia Americana, New Book of Knowledge, New Standard Encyclopedia, and World Book*."[6]

GENERAL TRENDS

Large media conglomerates have been in the process of selling off their reference, professional, and educational divisions in order to concentrate on consumer publishing. The converse of this trend is also true. Large conglomerates, in turn, are being formed which will focus on publishing reference, professional, and educational media. For example, Simon & Schuster has decided to concentrate on trade publishing while divesting itself of its other divisions like reference. At the same time, Thompson, now The Thompson Corporation (TTC), has been in the process of buying up respected publishers of reference, educational, and professional information like Gale, U·X·L, Simon & Schuster Reference, Macmillan Library Reference USA, Peterson's, and the Information Access Company (IAC), a company which has offered the enormous electronic and often full-text periodical resources of *InfoTrac* under the umbrella of *SearchBank*.

Publishers really seem to be listening to what their customers require and responding in kind. Many of them also seem to read the reviews of their products carefully and make improvements accordingly. Almost all reference publishers, large or small, seem to be committed to the quality of their content in order to keep a market share with dependable brand-name recognition. Publishers are also coming full circle. Instead of divesting themselves of trade holdings to streamline their operations, some like Facts On File are actually creating new trade imprints to broaden their markets.

Despite the explosion of online resources of a more scholarly nature, the reference book continues to thrive. More reference books are being published than ever before. Most of reference titles listed in this year's "Fall Reference Preview" of *Reference Books Bulletin* are available in print. Big multi-volume sets like Oxford's *American National Biography* (*ANB*) continue to be published first in print, though the *ANB* will soon migrate to the Web, just as Grove's *Dictionary of Art* has done.[7]

Electronic publishing is a very expensive proposition; and, therefore, it is difficult for smaller publishers to compete. By forming conglomerates, publishers can streamline their staff and let various divisions of their huge companies continue to do what they do best.

THE THOMPSON CORPORATION

The Thompson Corporation is a good paradigm for the ways in which publishers are repositioning themselves in the reference and educational markets. They formed The Gale Group as a subsidiary of Thompson Business Information. In September 1998 The Gale Group merged with the Information Access Company and now includes, among others, Primary Source Media, Graham and Whiteside, St. James Press, U·X·L, and The Taft Group. The name "Gale" was kept because it signifies a world-renowned publisher of reference and research material for academic, public, and school libraries as well as for professionals in education and business.

The Gale Group is now in the process of consolidating the comprehensive, serial, online resources of Information Access Company by bringing some of the Gale products online under a new name but under a name which has brand recognition, *InfoTrac Web Databases*. *Contemporary Authors, Contemporary Literary Criticism–Select, Expanded Academic Reference Index ASAP, Health Reference Center, General Reference Center, Predicasts PROMPT,* and the *General BusinessFile ASAP* are now available under the *InfoTrac Web Databases'* umbrella.

Brand name recognition has become an extremely important factor in both in the publishing of new books and the migration of respected publishers to online resources for both new and old publications. When conglomerates are formed, they prefer to keep the same names or the slightly changed names of their various divisions or subsidiaries, e.g., the Gale Group, Macmillan Library Reference, Simon & Schuster Reference, Peterson's, Twayne, and Charles Scribner's Sons because of their established name and prestige. A few years ago, Thompson tried to change the name of Gale Research to Information/Reference Group. The outcry from librarians and other customers was so great that Thompson reversed its decision and brought back the Gale name. Thompson learned a valuable lesson from that process. In the world of reference, the name is that which embodies a particular type of quality and content expected from a particular publisher.

This trend was already well in evidence by 1997. On May 12, 1997, just before the National Online Meeting in New York, a seminar, *Electronic Publishing XV,* jointly sponsored by the Information Industry Association and Information Today, Inc., was held. Executives in the publishing and information business met to discuss the future of electronic publishing trends. A thorough summary of issues and trends in electronic publishing with special emphasis on "branding" was presented:

1. Brand name value must transcend format
2. Interactivity (editorial involvement)
3. Customer relationships
4. Timeliness
5. Access to current and archival material
6. How to incorporate multimedia
7. Technology as added value, not as "sizzle"
8. Relationship to core product strategy[8]

CD-ROM AND ONLINE RESOURCES

Publishing trends in the CD-ROM market are being reformatted and diversified. Technology is changing on an almost minute-by-minute basis. In 1992 CD-ROMs were considered a "marvelous reference aid" and promised "to dominate the technology at reference centers in the decade ahead."[9] For the next five years, that was, indeed the case. By 1997, CD-ROM technology was still considered "reliable, easy to use, and almost impossible to pirate."[10] The first two parts of that statement are still true, but now there are affordable "burners" on the market that can replicate CD-ROMs. However, William Katz has always maintained that CD-ROM technology is a temporary, stopgap measure whose market will soon reach maturity. Technology had changed so rapidly that Katz has predicted that in the next decade online resources will replace the CD-ROM as an information device.[11] This prediction is already being fulfilled. Ulla de Stricker, in her paper for the proceedings of *Computers in Libraries '98*, has an informative chart entitled "CD-ROM Titles in Print" which seems to bear out Katz's assertions. In 1985, there were only two CD-ROM titles in print. Growth in the number of CD-ROM titles seemed to reach a high of 2.48% in 1989. Since then that growth has fluctuated from a high of 2.07% to a low in 1992 and 1998 of 1.42% with 27,000 CD-ROM titles in print in 1998 and a gradual decline in growth from 1996 on.[12]

The difficulty and expense of maintaining CD-ROMs on a network are contributing factors to their disfavor. CD-ROM servers are costly to maintain and installing weekly, monthly, or quarterly updates is a time-consuming and labor-intensive process–as each CD has its own proprietary method of installation, often having to be installed on each individual PC as well as on a network.

Online resources are often updated on a daily, hourly, or minute-by-minute basis with no effort on the part of the user. All the user requires is a PC and Internet access. Online services also make it much easier for the provider to make changes or enhancements. CD-ROMs used to be much less expensive than their online counterparts because the online versions offered the user greater currency. Now in order to entice users to the Web, publishers are offering the online version for the same price as or even less than the cost of a CD-ROM version. *SIRS Researcher's* and *SIRS Government Reporter's* online versions are now available from SIRS Mandarin at the same price as the CD-ROM; and the company, as many others are doing, is touting the CD-ROM for little or no extra cost as a backup when the online version is down. Online cataloging tools like *ITS.MARC* from TLC are updated daily and may offer periodic updates (quarterly, biannually, yearly) on CD-ROM as part of the cost of their online package. CD-ROMs have also been enhanced to attract users to the WEB. For example, *World Book Multimedia Encyclopedia* on CD-ROM is just one of many CD-ROMS that offer links to current news and article updates (formerly called "revisions" in print) on the Internet.

Smaller publishers of reference books seem to be less eager to go online and are still publishing new or reformatted information in both print and, to a lesser extent, on CD-ROM. Expense, to be sure, plays a large part in their ability to keep up with their bigger counterparts. They are managing to keep their share of the market by emphasizing the content and quality for which they are known, like Greenhaven Press with its *Opposing Viewpoints* series. Nevertheless, these small publishers are gradually realizing that in order to compete in the marketplace they, too, must develop online resources and Web sites, which will pay for themselves in the long run. Some of the smaller publishers are even conducting telephone surveys in order to better determine customer's needs.

FACTS ON FILE

Take Facts On File, one of the smaller publishers, for example. In the spring 1999 catalog, a letter to customers from Chairman Mark McDonnell states, "With each passing season at Facts On File, our primary goals remain the same: to develop even better and more relevant books, *On Files,* and CD-ROMs, and to offer you the best possible, quick and dependable service."[13] At that time, Facts On File seemed to be committed to publishing new reference sources in print and on CD-ROM as well as substantial revisions of their former best-sellers. By the fall of 1999, however, their CD-ROM offerings had been reduced from nine to eight, and the focus of the publisher has changed somewhat. In McDonnell's fall letter, using trite expressions like "catching the wave" and "rolling with technological advances," he now places the emphasis on online electronic resources.[14]

Facts On File is slowly joining the electronic age. In September 1999, Facts On File debuted a new web site (*http://www.factsonfile. com*) with the ability to browse its catalog by title, subject, series, or format, look at their suggestions for collection development by subject area, and order online. Because of popular demand, twenty-two of Facts On File's best selling *On File* binders will be available online for the first time. Their *African-American Multimedia Collection* on CD-ROM and *American Historical Images: An On-line Gallery* will also be available online this fall. Like many other publishers, large or small, Facts On File seems committed to publishing more timely and curriculum-driven reference works in print versions than ever before. Its literary offerings, *The Facts On File Companion to the American Short Story* and the *A to Z of American Women Writers* seem to bear this concept out. They are also continuing with substantial revisions of old favorites like the *Encyclopedia of Native American Tribes* and the *Dictionary of Wars.* Checkmark Books, Facts On File's new trade imprint, has also been successfully introduced, helped along by the long years of dependability which one has come to expect from books published under the Facts On File name.

PRESENT TRENDS AS INDICATORS OF FUTURE DEVELOPMENTS

The Thompson Corporation's 1998 annual report gives some interesting figures which are perhaps indicative of how the publishing market, especially a large conglomerate, views itself today and what the industry might offer in the future. The Thompson Corporation says that U. S. library reference is a $2.8 billion market and general reference, a $1.8 billion market. Annual growth for the academic library market is about 6% while the school and public library market's annual growth is about 4%. Thompson sees no overall growth in print formats but an 8% to 10% growth in the electronic products market. The library reference market, according to Thompson, is highly fragmented in the United States–hence the need for large conglomerates with the monetary resources to develop expensive electronic products.[15]

BELL & HOWELL INFORMATION AND LEARNING

Bell & Howell is another huge conglomerate that is acquiring companies and consolidating resources so as to be well-positioned in the market of the twenty-first century. Like many other companies, they are focusing on what they do well. Bell & Howell Information and Learning is the new name for UMI. However, their association is not new. UMI has had an affiliation with Bell & Howell since 1985. UMI started in 1938 with one product, the filming of original manuscripts of Early English literature in the British Museum. Since then they have collected and organized information from newspapers, out-of-print books, dissertations, and periodicals for universities, libraries, businesses, governments, and schools in over 160 countries. In fact, The Library of Congress has designated Bell & Howell Information and Learning's active electronic dissertations' and theses' collection as the official U. S. offsite repository for these items. Long the world leader in microfilm collections with rights to distribute that information, the company is now involved in the *Digital Vault Initiative*, converting its massive microfilm holdings of over 5.5 billion page images into digital format. Bell & Howell Information and Learning, however, had a headstart even on the *Digital Library Project*, which was first funded by the National Science Foundation in 1993. They had refined a system to reach agreements with thousands of publishers with regard to the payment of publishers and royalties to authors. Therefore, they are well placed to negotiate contracts for digital rights to additional products.[16]

The company specializes in two major brands: *UMI* for microform and print products and *ProQuest* for electronic products. Once again brand names, which have been long associated with offering content and quality for indexing and abstracting and for ASCII, full-text, facsimile, and full-imaged options, have been retained. Under the *UMI* name, resources like newspapers and periodicals in microform, print newspaper indexes, research collections, dissertation publishing, and books-on-demand are still available with an emphasis on archival qualities. Under the *ProQuest* name, there is a wide range of international business, career, technical, and educational databases online and on CD-ROM. *Digital Dissertations*, the *Digital Vault Initiative,* and value-added services like *SiteBuilder* are also offered.

In July 1999, Bell & Howell announced that they will join with Infonautics, Inc., pending regulatory and stockholder approval, to create a new company which will concentrate on the K-12 Internet market. *ProQuest* and *Electric Library*, two complementary and well-established Internet resources, will be the initial offerings of the new company. *Electric Library*, especially developed for schools and libraries in the K-12 market, is already in use in all 50 states by over 15,000 institutions. *Company Sleuth*, a free service from Infonautics, was named as one of the "Top 100 Web Sites" by *PC Magazine*. *Company Sleuth* searches the top job sites on the Internet and matches possibilities with a user's profile. This product will also be developed along with a new offering called "Sports Sleuth." The e-commerce online archive services provided to publishers and other "content creators" by Infonautics are certainly a useful complement to Bell & Howell's archival offerings.

The recent acquisition of Chadwyck-Healey is another great asset to Bell & Howell's stable of providers of backfile information. Since 1973 Chadwyck-Healey, which is based in the United Kingdom, has provided reference and full-text databases of a scholarly nature in areas like history, literature, political and social sciences, reference, and economics. They provide these products in a variety of formats: online, CD-ROM, and microfilm. Chadwyck-Healey is currently the leading publisher of online texts in the humanities, and their LION (Literature Online) and their PCI (Periodicals Contents Index) are innovative Web-based products. Once again, name recognition is of paramount importance. Bell & Howell will keep the Chadwyck-Healey name on many products because that name conveys a level of quality and content which customers come to expect.[17]

VALUE-ADDED SERVICES

Companies like Bell & Howell and The Thompson Corporation have also realized the benefit of value-added services to their customers. The ability of a user–whether it be a school, a library, or a business–to customize a site to its local needs and to integrate applications with its own resources, including an online catalog and third party vendors, is a definite attraction when choosing a publisher of electronic databases. Thompson's *InfoTrac* has *Total Access*, which allows access to all the digital resources a library or company may have. It also provides customized usage statistics, a library's or company's holdings information, and the ability to offer selected Web sites of the customer's choice. In a similar vein, Bell & Howell offers its own version, *ProQuest Direct SiteBuilder*, a "design your own interface." *SiteBuilder* permits table of contents access, article retrieval, integrated access, predefined searches, copyright-cleared information, and online access to usage reports and also gives access to course packs and predefined topic packages which are collections of articles and other resources, some from the *Digital Vault* collection. These course and topic packages are updated often to give the user the current information on a particular topic. *ProQuest Local Administrator* will provide local site administrators with a convenient method for managing their sites in-house.[18]

DEVELOPMENT OF K-12 RESOURCES

Like many other publishers, Thompson and Bell & Howell are developing databases and other resources for the K-12 population. Take Macmillan Library Reference USA (a division of Bell & Howell Information and Learning), for example. They are developing reference resources which are curriculum, budget, and age appropriate. Macmillan has taken older, more comprehensive reference sets and reformatted them into four volume sets which are suitable for high school students. *Latin America: History and Culture* is based on the award-winning *Encyclopedia of Latin American History and Culture*, and *Ancient Greece and Rome: An Encyclopedia for Students* is also designed for school students and is based on the three-volume *Civilization of the Ancient Mediterranean* and the two volume *Ancient Writers*. Macmillan's new compendiums are one volume works on various topics which are also derived from older, multi-volume sets. The compendium, *American History*, is drawn from the eight volume *Dictionary of American History* and its two volume supplement, and *Everyday Life: American Social History* from the three volume *Ency-*

clopedia of American Social History. Smaller publishers like Fitzroy Dearborn and Salem are also targeting school students either by offering titles appropriate for that age level and/or by offering substantial discounts on all their offerings. All types of formats of reference resources for upper elementary and high school students were previously scanty. Last year's fall preview in *Booklist* had difficulty coming up with twenty titles for that age group. This year, it was difficult to limit titles for that age group to twenty-five.[19]

NETLIBRARY

On March 29, 1999 netLibrary (*http://www.netlibrary.com*) instituted an Internet-based e-book service which will concentrate on furnishing scholarly, reference, and professional e-book services to public and academic libraries and to educational and business professionals. This privately held company, founded in 1998, has its headquarters in Boulder, Colorado.

Their goal is

> to work as a partner with libraries and publishers to serve higher education, K-12 education, distance learning and training organization, businesses, government agencies, and consumers with eBooks, multimedia enhancements, and data that will revolutionize learning and research.[20]

The growing trend of alliances and partnerships of groups of companies, publishers, libraries, and academic institutions is quite evident in the makeup of netLibrary. Quest Communications, the Anschutz Corporation, and Sequel Venture Partners are all investors in netLibrary. The Anschutz Corporation, one of the primary investors in Quest, is backed by billionaire Phillip Anschutz. The charter members of netLibrary include OhioLink, Palinet, the Colorado Alliance of Research Libraries, and the University of Texas. These library consortia represent over two million customers. OCLC will provide netLibrary with MARC cataloging, including 856 fields. This feature will allow libraries that are members of netLibrary and that have online catalogs to connect directly to netLibrary's e-books. NetLibrary has negotiated contracts to date with over seventy five respected and well-known commercial and university press publishers like ABC-CLIO, M. E.

Sharpe, Libraries Unlimited, Brookings Institution Press, Facts On File, the McGraw-Hill Companies, MIT Press, Stanford University Press, and Vanderbilt University Press. Currently reference titles offered include over 99 bibliographies and 24 dictionaries. This list will continue to grow as the site adds titles on a daily basis. At first, half the books will come from those available as public-domain titles from Project Gutenberg. NetLibrary, in turn, is helping to fund the Project Gutenberg to assure the project's continued operation. NetLibrary is aiming their market at larger libraries and will convert articles and books for which they have gained the rights of reproduction from print into netLibrary's proprietary digital format.

Many services which are available in libraries are also offered in netLibrary's virtual library. However, netLibrary services also include additional services like the ability to order books for a personal e-library in either print or e-book format at the retail price. Publishers will be reimbursed at the wholesale rate. NetLibrary will also generate revenue by offering customized usage statistics to publishers for marketing strategies and to libraries as an aid to collection development. Access to books in the public domain is free, and access to their private collection of copyrighted e-books is available at $29.95 per year. NetLibrary permits the downloading of e-books to a computer using their proprietary software, Knowledge Station. Hypertext searching by keyword, phrase, subject, author, or title, the ability to search thousands of texts simultaneously, print selected information as well as the ability to make notes and bookmarks are also attractive features of netLibrary. The electronic books can be "checked out" or viewed online.[21]

ARCHIVING

Archiving is another serious problem that must be addressed. Publishers are finally beginning to see that there is a market for publishing archival material in a digital format. Witness the *Digital Vault Initiative* of Bell & Howell or netLibrary's e-book initiative. However, because the Internet and the World Wide Web are changing so fast, publishers barely have time to consider archiving present materials. Will the back issues of e-journals and Internet/electronic database resources still be available in the future? For example, some Web sites reviewed last year in *Library Journal* have already disappeared from the Web. Magnetic tape has a life span of about five to seven years. CD-ROMs have an archival life span of about twenty-five to fifty years, while online there are thousands of innovations being introduced on an almost minute-by-minute basis. Who knows which of these innovations will survive, and whether older resources will still be accessible five or ten years from now? Will the computer hardware necessary to use the information stored on today's technology continue to exist? Witness the difficulty in finding a computer with a drive which can read the old 5 1/4 inch floppy disks. Many publishers have developed a "rotating" archival coverage. As the current year is added to a database, the oldest year of coverage is dropped. Currently the range is five to seven years. The articles that are dropped are then "lost" to the subscribers of that particular database.

COPYRIGHT

Copyright issues present another concern for electronic databases. On the positive side, large conglomerates have the resources to negotiate various copyright agreements with publishers of serials as well as individual authors, making it much easier for the consumer to deal with one vendor instead of many–a kind of "one-stop shopping." Some publishers like Bell & Howell have a significant advantage in the marketplace because of the fact that they already own the copyright to a very large collection of archival material.

The downside is that these copyright agreements are in a constant state of flux. Copyrights to various journals and fair use agreements are constantly being negotiated with the result that the article which a user accessed yesterday may not be there today because a company has lost the rights to publish it. The *ProQuest Direct* or *EbscoHost* of today is not the *ProQuest Direct* or *EbscoHost* of tomorrow.

TECHNOLOGY'S FUTURE

Perhaps the Information Age is not really so different after all. One may remember the impermanence of the papyri of the Greeks and the Romans or the lost books of Livy. The ability to read the hieroglyphics of the ancient Egyptians was lost to us until the discovery of the

Rosetta Stone by an engineer in Napoleon's army and its subsequent decipherment by Champollion. In the past, war, natural disasters, or religious intolerance were just a few of the reasons why the written word perished. Today we have added technology to the cauldron.

Some new technologies are accepted immediately, and others will be resisted or even rejected because of a 'momentum of ideas' that allows opinions, attitudes, and beliefs to take on a life of their own, both in individuals and in groups. This 'momentum of ideas' shapes the world just as much as do historical circumstances, scientific knowledge, and the technological infrastructure.[22] Whether or not the momentum of the idea of the Internet's influence on society will rival that of the printing press remains to be seen. However, just as when Gutenberg introduced the printing press, he chose to reproduce his books as facsimiles of manuscripts, so too, have the Internet, on-line catalogs, and electronic databases tried to model themselves on what is currently familiar. The way in which information will be presented in the future remains in question and may well change drastically from anything now imagined. "The inventing of the printing press in the 1400s and the resulting spread of information created an unparalleled change in western society . . . It is not a large leap to conclude that the Internet will open up a new era in human history, whose characteristics we can only guess."[23] We often base decisions about technology and its future prospects on yesterday's and not today's technology and that many influences–social, political, cultural, economic, etc.–shape technology just as much as or sometimes even more than engineering and scientific principles.

LIBRARIES

Libraries continue to grow steadily, but often a smaller staff is asked to do more. The enormous number of electronic databases, both available from information providers for a fee and those that are free on the Internet, offers very little in the way of standardization. Users seem to want quality but not quantity, yet we are being inundated with information, much of which is misinformation or information of a frivolous nature. Sound evaluation of reference sources will become even more critical as the Internet and the World Wide Web continue to grow. We have seen the rise of e-journals, interlibrary loan at the click of a mouse, full-text databases both on-line and on

CD-ROM, and more recently, databases that can be downloaded onto a client's own server. However, the problems of copyright and licensing are complex and must be addressed soon. Old rules no longer apply.

Libraries are fighting back. Not only are libraries forming consortia with other libraries, they are forming consortia with scholarly and commercial presses. SPARC (Scholarly Publishing and Academic Resources Coalition), founded by the Association of Research Libraries, uses funds pledged by members to support and subsidize publishers of e-journals so that they can compete with more costly commercial publications. Library consortia which were once formed for the sharing of their catalogs are now in the business of negotiating contracts and licensing agreements with publishers in order to obtain the most favorable usage rights and cost for their members.

Some individual states have had the foresight to plan the organization of dissemination of information in their states through their libraries. For example, the Massachusetts Library Commission, through a network of regional library systems, has implemented a plan to give equal access to a full range of services and electronic databases.

THE "HAVES" AND THE "HAVE NOTS"

New technologies are everywhere but are more pervasive in some countries than others. President Clinton is always talking about getting every American access to the Information Superhighway. Bill Gates and Steve Jobs are helping to make this dream happen with large infusions of money to bring public libraries online. EBSCO Publishing and George Soros's Open Society Institute (OSI) have initiated an innovative resource, Electric Information for Libraries Direct (EIFL Direct), that focuses on bringing information to thirty-nine information-deficient countries of Central and Eastern Europe as well as Haiti and Guatemala. Over 3,200 full-text magazines, newspapers, scholarly journals, newswires, and 1,300 full-text brochures and reference books will be available to academic, medical, national, public, and research libraries. Depending on the level of technology, EIFL Direct users will access these databases via the Web, CD-ROM, or DVD-ROM.[24]

Despite these initiatives and promises to bring technology to the disadvantaged, the gap between the "haves" and the "have-nots" is increasing. Like the promise of "a chicken in every pot," a slogan used in the 1928 American presidential campaign and before that by Henry of Navarre, these promises may not be feasible or even realistic. The global village envisioned by Marshall McLuhan is fast becoming a village of "haves," the technologically developed countries, and the "have-nots," consisting of Third World countries and the poor of developed countries. Countries may well not be made in their own image but in the image of those with the technological power. If Third World countries are finally able to acquire some of that technological power, will it be in the hands of the few for their own personal benefit as has often been the case in the past? How will the poor, the homeless, and the disadvantaged get online when many of them don't even have electricity, homes to go to, or money to buy the necessary hardware? Libraries, especially public libraries, will be one of the few places where they will be able to go for information and for help in acquiring the services they need. The idea of a virtual library could work well for the "haves" but will not be possible for the poor who will still need a physical place to go for information. The expense of online resources and hardware is often prohibitive, and libraries must be better funded globally by both the public and private sectors if there is to be any hope for the "have-nots." Perhaps, we will see electronic services made readily available in shelters and in service-oriented organizations as adjuncts to those services already offered by libraries.

The kaleidoscope, which is the publishing business, is changing so rapidly that it is becoming a blur of confusing offerings and options. The economy is currently in good shape so there is money available to support research and development. Who can say what will happen once we hit a recession? This has become the age of customization: customized user and licensing agreements, customized pricing, customized local sites, and customized deals of every sort. This puzzling array of offerings and technology must begin to stabilize if the innovations of today are going to survive. Many of these innovations will indeed disappear, and the ones that survive will be shaped, perhaps, more by social, political, economic, and cultural aspects than by the technology itself. More and more reference resources will continue to go online; but, unless prices drop significantly, only "the few" will have the resources to purchase them. We are seeing scholars making deals directly with online aggregators of information in order to give their work greater exposure, thus cutting out the third party publisher. Libraries and businesses are following suit.

Are librarians, as David Majka suggests in his null hypothesis, bringing a Trojan horse into their midst because of their wide acceptance and promulgation of full-text periodical databases? Will publishers cut out the third party, i.e., the library, and sell directly to the consumer at a greatly reduced rate, effectively taking libraries out of the loop?[25] Inexpensive scholarly databases like *Electric Library* are already sold directly to the public. Instead of taking business away from libraries, the library market for these types of databases has grown, and large conglomerates continue to view the school and library market as a place for growth. Despite what Majka says, libraries, for the most part, are already "acting collectively, marketing effectively, and drawing upon each others collection strengths at the speed that patrons demand and expect."[26]

More and more of our information is being controlled by fewer and fewer publishers. How this situation will affect the quality, the accuracy, and the content of information in the future remains to be seen. We must be vigilant that subliminal as well as obvious suggestions and ideas from the few not skew our collective and personal views.

Libraries have come a long way since S. R. Ranganathan laid down his Five Laws of Library Science: books are for use, every book its reader, every reader his book, save time of the reader, and the library is a growing organism. Yet, libraries may not really be so different after all. Ranganathan's five principles have endured the test of time. Although perhaps for the word "book," we need to substitute those inelegant, jargon words "multiple formats." But, the idea is the same. His last principle is like a shining beacon, illuminating the past and lighting the path ahead. The library is still a growing organism–growing in strange and wondrous ways that Ranganathan may have never foreseen. Predictions of the death of the library and the book have been greatly exaggerated. As we embark on the new millennium, libraries and librarians can be proud of the fact that they have not remained complacent and stagnant, that they have, for the most part, kept pace with new developments in technology and will continue to work with the publishers in innovative and creative ways. This time the publishers are listening. Libraries and librarians will survive, changed to be sure, but no less committed to the quality and content of the resources we provide.

NOTES

1. For an excellent survey of Internet history, see Christos J. P. Moschovitis . . . [et al]. *History of the Internet: A Chronology 1843 to the Present.* Santa Barbara, CA: ABC-CLIO, 1999.

2. "Two Indicative Events In the History of Book Publishing." *digital publishing technologies: dpt*, August 1999: 1.

3. Sottong, Stephen. "Don't Power Up That E-book Just Yet." *American Libraries*, vol. 30, no. 5, May 1999: 50-53.

4. "Two Indicative Events:" 1.

5. Katz, William A. *Introduction to Reference Work, Volume I: Basic Information Sources*, 7th edition. New York: McGraw-Hill, 1997: 211.

6. Quinn, Mary Ellen. "Encyclopedia Update, 1999." *Booklist*. vol. 96, no. 2, September 1999: 278.

7. Quinn, Mary Ellen. "Fall Reference Preview." *Booklist*, vol. 95, no. 22, August 1999: 2076.

8. Erickson, Cara as reported by Paula J. Hane. "Defining the Future of Digital Publishing." *Information Today*. vol. 14, no. 7, July/August 1997: 47. EbscoHost: *Academic Search Elite*. Accession no. 9709175012. 1 November 1999.

9. Katz, William A. *Introduction to Reference Work, Volume II: Reference Services and Reference Processes*, 6th edition. New York: McGraw-Hill, 1992: 130.

10. Katz, William A. *Introduction to Reference Work, Volume II: Reference Services and Reference Processes*, 7th edition. New York: McGraw-Hill, 1997: 55, footnote 33.

11. Katz: 55, footnote 33.

12. de Stricker, Ulla. "New Information Technologies: Possible Implications for Libraries." *Computers In Libraries '98: Proceedings.* (Arlington, VA, March 2-4, 1998). Medford, NJ: Information Today, 1998: 55.

13. *Spring Catalog 1999.* Facts On File, 1999: 1.

14. *Fall Catalog 1999-2000.* Facts On File, 1999: 1.

15. "Fundamentals: Reference, Science, & Healthcare." *The Thompson Corporation 1998 Annual Report.* [Online]. Available: *http://www.thomcorp.com/annua198/16-17-ref-sci-health.html.* 16 November 1999.

16. For more information on the *Digital Vault Project*, see Peter Jasco. "UMI's Digital Vault Initiative Project." *Information Today*, vol. 15, no. 8, September 1998. [Online]. Available: *http://www.infotoday.com/it/sep98/jacso.htm.*16 November 1999.

17. Reynolds, Joe, CEO of Bell & Howell Information and Learning, in a press release entitled, "Bell & Howell Acquires Chadwyck-Healey." [Online]. Available: *http://www.umi.com/hp/PressRel/990929.html.* 16 November 1999.

18. For more information see *SiteBuilder.* [Online]. Available: *http://www.umi.com/hp/Features/SiteBuilder/.*

19. Quinn, Mary Ellen. "Fall Reference Preview." *Booklist*, August 1999, v. 95, issue 22: 2706.

20. "Who We Are." netLibrary. [Online]. Available: *http://www.netlibrary.com/who.asp.* 16 November 1999.

21. For more information on netLibrary see *http://www.netlibrary.com* and David Dorman. "Technically speaking." *American Libraries*, vol. 30, no. 4, April 1999: 90.

22. Pool, Robert. *Beyond Engineering: How Society Shapes Technology.* New York: Oxford University Press, 1997: 54.

23. Pool: 56.

24. Rogers, Michael. "EBSCO and OSI creating Global Library Consortium." *Library Journal*, vol. 124, no. 18, November 1, 1999: 27.

25. Majka, David R. "Of Portals, Publishers, and Privatization." *American Libraries*, vol. 30, no. 9, October 1999: 44.

26. Majka: 49.

BIBLIOGRAPHY

de Stricker, Ulla. "New Information Technologies: Possible Implications for Libraries." *Computers In Libraries '98: Proceedings.* (Arlington, VA, March 2-4, 1998). Medford, NJ: Information Today, 998: 52-56.

Dorman, David. "Technically speaking." *American Libraries*, vol. 30, no. 4, April 1999: 90.

Erickson, Cara as reported by Paula J. Hane. "Defining the Future of Digital Publishing." *Information Today.* vol. 14, no. 7, July/August 1997: 47. EbscoHost: *Academic Search Elite.* Accession no. 9709175012.

Fall Catalog 1999-2000. Facts On File, 1999.

"Fundamentals: Reference, Science, & Healthcare." *The Thompson Corporation 1998 Annual Report.* [Online]. Available: *http://www.thomcorp.com/annua198/16-17-ref-sci-health.html.*

Jasco, Peter. "UMI's Digital Vault Initiative Project." *Information Today*, vol. 15, no. 8, September 1998. [Online]. Available: *http://www.infotoday.com/it/sep98/jacso.htm.*

Katz, William A. *Introduction to Reference Work, Volume I: Basic Information Sources,* 7th edition. New York: McGraw-Hill, 1997.

Katz, William A. *Introduction to Reference Work, Volume II: Reference Services and Reference Processes,* 6th edition. New York: McGraw-Hill, 1992.

Katz, William A. *Introduction to Reference Work, Volume II: Reference Services and Reference Processes,* 7th edition. New York: McGraw-Hill, 1997.

Majka, David R. "Of Portals, Publishers, and Privatization." *American Libraries*, vol. 30, no. 9, October 1999: 46-49.

Moschovitis, Christos J. P. . . . [et al]. *History of the Internet: A Chronology 1843 to the Present.* Santa Barbara, CA: ABC-CLIO, 1999.

netLibrary. [Online]. Available: *http://www.netlibrary.com.*

Pool, Robert. *Beyond Engineering: How Society Shapes Technology.* New York: Oxford University Press, 1997.

Quinn, Mary Ellen. "Encyclopedia Update, 1999." *Booklist.* vol. 96, no. 2, September 1999: 278-300.

Quinn, Mary Ellen. "Fall Reference Preview." *Booklist*, vol. 95, no. 22, August 1999: 2076-2102.

Reynolds, Joe, CEO of Bell & Howell Information and Learning, in a press release entitled, "Bell & Howell Acquires Chadwyck-Healey." [Online]. Available: *http://www.umi.com/hp/PressRel/990929.html.*

Rogers, Michael. "EBSCO and OSI creating Global Library Consortium." *Library Journal*, vol. 124, no. 18, November 1, 1999: 27.

SiteBuilder. [Online]. Available: *http://www.umi.com/hp/Features/SiteBuilder/*.

Spring Catalog 1999. Facts On File, 1999.

Sottong, Stephen. "Don't Power Up That E-book Just Yet." *American Libraries*, vol. 30, no. 5, May 1999: 50-53.

"Two Indicative Events In the History of Book Publishing." *digital publishing technologies: dpt*, August 1999: 1.

"Who We Are." netLibrary. [Online]. Available: *http://www.netlibrary.com/who.asp.*

Information Literacy
in the Reference Environment:
Preparing for the Future

Hannelore B. Rader

SUMMARY. The academic information environment is changing greatly as we enter the millennium. These changes are affecting libraries and specifically, reference services. In the past and even in recent times librarians have been concerned with library orientation, library instruction and bibliographic instruction. Now they have to worry about teaching students and others viable information and computer skills to cope effectively in the information society. Reference work as practiced this century will undergo major changes in the electronic information environment and the teaching of effective information skills will become a very important component of reference services. The challenges thus presented to academic librarians will be great but success in this area will mean effective professional survival. *[Article copies available for a fee from The Haworth Document Delivery Service: 1-800-342- 9678. E-mail address: <getinfo@haworthpressinc.com> Website: <http://www.HaworthPress.com>]*

KEYWORDS. Information skills, information literacy, teaching, reference service, electronic information, professional survival

---

Hannelore B. Rader is University Librarian, Ekstrom Library, University of Louisville, Louisville, KY 40292 (E-mail: h.rader@louisville.edu).

This article is based on the author's earlier publication "Reference Services as a Teaching Function" (*Library Trends*, 1980) and on many years of experience both in reference and information literacy.

[Haworth co-indexing entry note]: "Information Literacy in the Reference Environment: Preparing for the Future." Rader, Hannelore B. Co-published simultaneously in *The Reference Librarian* (The Haworth Information Press, an imprint of The Haworth Press, Inc.) No. 71, 2000, pp. 25-33; and: *New Technologies and Reference Services* (ed: Bill Katz) The Haworth Information Press, an imprint of The Haworth Press, Inc., 2000, pp. 25-33. Single or multiple copies of this article are available for a fee from The Haworth Document Delivery Service [1-800-342-9678, 9:00 a.m. - 5:00 p.m. (EST). E-mail address: getinfo@ haworthpressinc.com].

Making information available is not enough. Making information useful is the key. Personalized attention, training, and after service responsiveness are now competitive requirements. Using communication and information technologies to make people more information literate is a viable approach.[1]

INTRODUCTION

Technology and the electronic information explosion are having a major impact on society as a whole; business, education, and libraries in particular. People need new skills to learn and to cope with the expanding information in their lives. They need to acquire these new skills and learn how to obtain, evaluate and apply information to solve problems and address important issues in the workplace and in their daily lives. There are no definitive methods to address these information dilemmas although businesses, schools, post secondary institutions and libraries are attempting to offer solutions and training. Helping people to be successful in finding and using information in the electronic environment is an extremely complex process. Public and academic library users now want efficient and effective one-stop shopping in a seamless access environment. They do not want to read complicated manuals, study the complexities of databases, or know about complicated search mechanisms. To deal with this situation, librarians have to provide library systems designed to facilitate access and information skills instruction at the time of need. Reference services are especially affected by these new needs and demands in the electronic information environment and reference librarians will have to rethink their service goals and outcomes fairly quickly to stay viable in this highly competitive information environment.

HISTORY

Discussions about reference service and what exactly it should entail have been documented in the library literature and conferences since the late 19th century. These discussions often address reference service as a teaching function and provide rationale for it.[2] This trend has been especially strong in the 1980's and the 1990's. Charles Bunge provided a thorough definition and theory for reference services and its relationship to library instruction from the 19th century to the 1980's and explains the role of the reference librarians as learning advisor and information facilitator. He also discusses the impact of computer applications and the need for good planning and evaluation of reference services.[3] Kathleen Gunning provided a thought-provoking discussion regarding the impact of user instruction and computer searching programs on reference. Results found more complex organizational structures, additional training needs for reference librarians and more fully integrated public service programs.[4] Advocates of an integrated public service model including computer searching and user instruction programs made their ideas clear to their fellow professionals at the ACRL Third National Conference in Seattle in 1984. Several papers addressed extended reference services models in order to provide reference services in a complex environment and changing user needs.[5] Throughout the historical development of reference services discussions have occurred on a regular basis whether or not library instruction should be a part of reference services. Many librarians have felt that guidance and instruction of library users occur regularly in reference work on an individual basis and group instruction is a natural progression. Although throughout the last three decades several academic libraries incorporated bibliographic instruction into reference services, this did not become a major trend and organizational issues often clouded the service mandates.

PRESENT SITUATION

Libraries have been part of a major information revolution for more than a decade and must now rethink all their functions, services as well as their organizational structure. Increasingly, the impact of the electronic information environment and the constantly changing technology are forcing librarians to deal with major changes. While librarians have to remain in a continuous learning mode to keep up with new trends and sources they must rethink how they do their work and how they provide their services. Traditionally, librarians have provided information and reference services on their terms and expected users to abide by those terms. However, now librarians must begin to understand the changing desires and needs of their users as related to acquiring knowledge and using information. More and more people now have access to computers, at work, at home or in school. They are experiencing immediate information access and delivery through the Internet and expect the same quick results from libraries. They may, however, need guidance, advice and instruction in getting the specific information they need and want, especially, in handling the information effectively and critically. A study at Duke University to ascertain the library model of the future found among a variety of other things that people characterize a good information source as:

- Accessible
- Fast
- Labor saving
- Free
- Computerized
- Networked with other libraries
- Comprehensive
- Available expertise[6]

These findings are important for viable and successful reference services and librarians are beginning to experiment with new and different types of reference services. Most of these services are integrating various new or non-traditional activities in creative ways to address user needs.

- Users need help with technology so "help desk" pieces are becoming parts of reference services.
- Users need instruction in accessing, organizing and using information, so information literacy is being incorporated into reference services.
- Users need help remotely, so electronic communication, including video conferencing is integrated into reference work.
- Users want assistance at their location, so reference librarians often roam around the library to accommodate these needs, or they go to faculty offices to provide needed services.

Changes and innovations are needed fast because of competition from information technology, vendors, the World Wide Web, and other types of information providers. The changes are also needed because of pressures from funding sources, accrediting groups and administrative mandates. Yet these changes are difficult and slow to implement because they will have to overcome traditional services and mind sets. Librarians have performed reference services in a certain manner for many years, they have not been trained to perform some of the new services and frankly, some are not eager to change.

The impact of technology on reference services and bibliographic instruction continues to be discussed in various publications but usually separately not in an integrated mode. Although strong relationships and connections are described between bibliographic instruction and reference services, the impact of technology on the two is usually treated separately.[7]

The evolving electronic environment has certainly influenced both reference services and bibliographic instruction. The need for librarians in academic as well as public libraries is documented by the fact that library users now often need professional help and guidance in the chaos and overabundance of electronic publications. In recent years, it has become more obvious that public librarians similar to academic librarians need to offer instruction in information skills to their clientele. Users of academic as well as public libraries need expert help and instruction in order to navigate through the World Wide Web and the multitude of other electronic information formats. Librarians are the expert professionals in the current complex information environment to assist people with their information needs within a carefully selected collection of resources, in an open, equitable access environment and at no cost. Library professionals are closely tied to the principles of democracy allowing freedom of choice, access to all types of views and thoughts and offering life-long learning opportunities.[8]

In January 1998 the Library of Congress sponsored an Institute on *Reference Service in a Digital Age* (http://lcweb.loc.gov/rr/digiref/ neworlns.html) in New Orleans during the meeting of the American Library Association. Presentations and discussions centered on the role of reference in the electronic environment and how to prepare for the future. A variety of scenarios were described from traditional reference desk models to reference service in a totally remote video conferencing environment. Most of the scenarios included some type of user instruction on a one-on-one basis. Reference librarians now are called upon not only to supply expert advice, training and assistance with information questions but also with technological and networking problems.

During the Institute it became clear that reference services in whatever format will continue to be needed in the electronic environment and that librarians, because of their training and experience with information, are uniquely qualified to provide these services. Human interaction in the reference environment will continue to be important and necessary for successful information assistance. Training and development for librarians will be mandatory for them to stay current in their reference work.

The expertise gained through the Internet Public Library, begun in 1995 at the University of Michigan, demonstrates that librarians need to

- set clear guidelines for electronic reference services,
- build close cooperation among reference librarians,
- identify remote clientele and their needs,
- obtain extensive training and development.

The Interactive Reference Service at the University of California Irvine describes how reference service was expanded beyond the reference desk using video teleconferencing technology *(http://www.ala. org/acrl/paperhtm/a10.html)*. This type of service will be an effective substitute for distance problems in communication and personal user-librarian interaction. The experiment is important so that it can be ascertained

- how desktop video teleconferencing can provide remote reference services
- how reliable is such technology
- how effective is the communication between librarians and clients
- how such technology can be integrated into regular reference service
- how this service will affect staffing
- how to instruct the users of this service.

There are several challenges librarians will have to address in the desktop video teleconferencing reference service. These challenges involve communication etiquette, training, technical problem solving and others. The experiment at UC Irvine will be well worth watching.

The present reference and instruction environment is definitely in a state of flux. Basically stated, reference services provide the human touch in guiding information users in the digital environment while information literacy (an expanded bibliographic instruction) is the most critical enabler for lifelong learning and effective information use. In the digital information environment reference services and information skills instruction need to become integrated to offer library users and information seekers the most convenient and supportive learning environment. In fact, integrating these two important public service components in libraries will ensure that librarians remain a viable and important sector of the information and education environment.

THE FUTURE

As librarians prepare for the millennium reference and instruction services will increasingly gain importance if the following factors are considered

- realistic assessment of users' needs and requirements
- user convenience
- availability of integrated and well-functioning information technology
- efficient assistance with technology
- available network of subject expertise
- expert information guidance in libraries and remotely
- quick and convenient instruction in information skills.

Limited availability of user survey data indicates that people generally are used to one-stop shopping and expect similar convenience from libraries. Information is wanted quickly, seamlessly and with expert human guidance. These expectations constitute a major challenge for librarians who have usually provided services at their convenience, not always quickly nor seamlessly. Rethinking and realigning will probably have to occur from the way libraries are organized, to how quickly they place information into their customers' hands and to what extent they use customer service attitudes. Each one of the service parts needs to be scrutinized and conceivably changed. That is hard and very challenging work in the complex library and technology environment.

INTEGRATION OF USER INSTRUCTION AND REFERENCE

To integrate user instruction and reference services the organizational structure would have to be changed so that librarians would have responsibilities in various professional areas such as reference, instruction, collections and technology. This would necessitate major training and development initiatives for the staff; perhaps as much as 5-10% of staff time might have to be allocated to training for a period of time. In addition to their professional training, librarians would need people and teaching skills, knowledge of print and electronic databases, basic technology and networking skills and knowledge of information sources in the surrounding areas. Librarians would have to build partnerships with teaching faculty, computer experts, and other information specialists to provide the best information access for their clientele.

Information skills instruction can be provided as needed on an individual basis or in groups. Such instruction needs to be convenient and to the point. Depending on user needs, it can be

- in person,
- interactively online,
- in print, or
- in an electronic classroom situation.

It is during the reference process that librarians actually determine the user's needs for information skills. During the reference interview, librarians can assess whether or not a customer has the skills to access information, evaluate it, collect it and use it. It is at that point that the reference librarian can offer and supply necessary instruction in these areas. Some users may need simple computer skills, some may need Internet instruction and many of them will need to learn about different types of information sources.

As librarians work in partnerships with others and, perhaps in team environments, they will be able to provide reference and instruction services as needed by the clients. However, changes in organizations and services take time and are difficult to institute. For example, the selection and implementation of an up-to-date library automation system is a costly and time-consuming process, as is organizational change to partnerships and teamwork, a process that could take several years.

Unfortunately, librarians do not have a great deal of time to accomplish some of the changes. Technology is forcing institutions and organizations including libraries to move more quickly to respond to change. Competition in the information environment is adding to the pressure. Funding issues and new information supply models are also having a major impact.

The good thing is that librarians are uniquely qualified and trained to address these challenges and to provide the type of information and instruction services needed and desired by their clientele. Librarians have many talents, and they have a reputation for providing good, reliable service to all people. Librarians are uniquely positioned to provide these important information and instruction services in the next century and to become a significant component of the information age.

REFERENCES

1. Karen T. Quinn, "Information Literacy in the Workplace: Education/Training Considerations." Information Literacy. Learning How to Learn, edited by Jana Varlejs. Jefferson, NC: McFarland, 1991, 19.

2. Hannelore B. Rader, "Reference Services as a Teaching Function," *Library Trends* (Summer, 1980):95-103.

3. Bunge, Charles A, "The Personal Touch. A Brief Overview of the Development of Reference Services in American Libraries," *Reference Service: A Perspective*, edited by Sul Lee. Ann Arbor, MI: Pierian Press, 1983, 1-16.

4. Gunning, Kathleen, "The Impact of User Education and Computer Service Programs on Reference Services," *Reference Services: A Perspective*, edited by Sul Lee. Ann Arbor, MI: Pierian Press, 1983: 79-88.

5. Martell, Charles R. et al. "A House Divided: Public Services Realities in the 1980's," *Proceedings of the ACRL Third National Conference*. Chicago: American Library Association, 1984, 85-101.

6. Campbell, Jerry D., "In Search of New Foundations for Reference," *Rethinking Reference in Academic Libraries*, edited by Anne G. Lipow. Berkeley, CA: Library Solutions Press, 1993, 3-1.

7. Sager, Harvey, "Implications for Bibliographic Instruction," *The Impact of Emerging Technologies on Reference Service and Bibliographic Instruction*, edited by Gary M. Pitkin. Westport, CN: Greenwood Press, 1995, 49-62.

8. Lipow, Anne G., "Thinking Out Loud. Who Will Give Reference Service in the Digital Environment," *Reference and User Services Quarterly 37* (Winter, 1997): 125-129.

WORKING AT REFERENCE

If We Hold It, Will They Come?
Searching Sessions at SUNY New Paltz

Susan Kraat

SUMMARY. With each technological leap, Bibliographic Instruction librarians are seeking innovative ways to reach users. Reference librarians at the State University of New York at New Paltz implemented a series of drop-in workshops during the Fall Semester of 1997. The sessions were designed to help students with searching skills, using the OPAC, ERIC on CD-ROM, SearchBank online database, and the Internet. A new electronic classroom was constructed to provide an interactive environment for the classes. The purpose of this study was to study data collected at the time of the workshops and to ask whether non-mandatory sessions have a viable place in a library instruction program. Should the workshops be repeated, and how might they be more effective? The study further proposed to examine how these and other forms of instruction might fit into a college wide program of information literacy.

Librarians who worked on the project were interviewed. They answered questions concerning the objectives of the sessions and whether those goals were met. In addition, they offered suggestions for im-

Susan Kraat is Reference Librarian, State University of New York, New Paltz, NY 12561.

[Haworth co-indexing entry note]: "If We Hold It, Will They Come? Searching Sessions at SUNY New Paltz." Kraat, Susan. Co-published simultaneously in *The Reference Librarian* (The Haworth Information Press, an imprint of The Haworth Press, Inc.) No. 71, 2000, pp. 35-58; and: *New Technologies and Reference Services* (ed: Bill Katz) The Haworth Information Press, an imprint of The Haworth Press, Inc., 2000, pp. 35-58. Single or multiple copies of this article are available for a fee from The Haworth Document Delivery Service [1-800-342-9678, 9:00 a.m. - 5:00 p.m. (EST). E-mail address: getinfo@haworthpressinc.com].

35

provement and opinions concerning mandatory instruction. Administrators discussed progress towards an institutional commitment to a college wide Information Literacy effort.

Workshop participants were asked to complete a survey at the end of each "Super Searching Session." Requested information included the type of workshop attended; grade status; whether they were a transfer, adult, or international student; how they learned about the workshops; and if they felt the classes were helpful. The number of students attending was low, despite extensive marketing efforts. Results of these surveys indicate greater attendance by upper level undergraduates and graduate students. A high number of attendees were transfer and adult students.

College committees and roundtables have been created to explore ways of meeting the Middle States standards for Information Literacy. In addressing the desire for students to have a "meaningful encounter with technology" while at New Paltz, administrators discuss issues such as required courses; discipline-specific courses that incorporate computer and/or information literacy; the role of the library; cooperation of faculty, library, and computer services. A university-wide initiative that would nurture the beginnings of such "meaningful encounters," must be the first step towards an institutional program of Information Literacy. *[Article copies available for a fee from The Haworth Document Delivery Service: 1-800-342-9678. E-mail address: <getinfo@haworthpressinc.com> Website: <http://www.HaworthPress.com>]*

KEYWORDS. Bibliographic instruction, computer literacy, searching online

INTRODUCTION

Shall I compare thee to a summer's day?
Thou art more lovely and more temperate.
Rough winds do shake the darling buds of May,
And summer's lease hath all too short a date.
Sometimes too hot the eye of heaven shines,
And often is his gold complexion dimmed.
And every fair from fair sometime declines,
By chance or Nature's changing course untrimmed:
But thy eternal summer shall not fade
Nor lose possession of that fair thou ow'st,
Nor shall Death brag thou wand'rest in his shade
When in eternal lines to time thou grow'st.
   So long as men can breathe or eyes can see,
   So long lives this, and this gives life to thee. (Shakespeare 38)

Shakespeare's sonnet affirms the permanence of the written word at each reading. For centuries the poem has existed in print, accessible by simply opening a book. Today, those same words can also be read on a database or on the Internet through the manipulation of clusters of 0's and 1's.

The familiar world of the print resource has changed. Speculating on the future of reading and technology, George Steiner writes: "Periods of transition are difficult to make out. They are also intensely stimulating . . . The conception of the planet as a living book, as a single storehouse of information, record, entertainment, rhetorical argument–each special domain interrelated with all others via electronic synapses of recognition, classification, and translation (as in the human brain?)–is no longer a science-fiction fantastication" (Steiner 120). It is not easy to predict when today's electronic revolution will end, and what libraries will be like even ten years from today. However, it is obvious that the dizzying onslaught of electronic gewgaws have catapulted librarians into the limelight. Librarians have always sought to bring patron and information together in the most meaningful way possible. That task has become increasingly complex as the capability to store and transmit vast amounts of information has soared to unimaginable heights. Dorothy might say to Toto, "Databases come and go so quickly here!" were she a reference librarian in any academic library of the 1990's.

Now is the time for academic librarians to maximize the importance of their role as navigators through this digital universe. Bibliographic instructors in particular continually search for new ways to teach students the skills they will need for the workplace. To that end reference librarians at the State University of New York at New Paltz developed a series of drop-in workshops for the convenience of students and faculty. In evaluating those workshops the researcher asks:

1. Does this format fit into the bibliographic instruction program?
2. How could such workshops be more effective?
3. How do these and other forms of bibliographic instruction fit into a university-wide program of Information Literacy?

If Tom Eadie and others maintain that library user education is of questionable worth, they should spend an hour with Barbara Petruzzelli. Petruzzelli, Assistant Director of the Sojourner Truth Library at New Paltz, takes an evangelical approach towards the need for required bibliographic instruction: "You cannot wait for the student to come to you. If you wait until students are ready to start their paper, it's too late. Students perceived point of need is always too late. Voluntary instruction cannot be left up to them . . . how many of them would take English Comp if they didn't' have to?" (Petruzzelli 7 July).

Petruzzelli was one of four reference librarians who taught the drop-in workshops, during the Fall 1997 Semester. Sixty-seven users participated in the Super Searching Sessions, which were designed to enhance searching skills. Why this hands-on environment, which required considerably more expense than classes conducted in a demonstration format? Was the outcome worth the time and effort and money spent? The librarian instructors, the Library Director, and the Vice President for Academic Affairs, speak to these issues, and to the larger issue of information literacy in a series of personal interviews.

THE PURPOSE OF THE STUDY

- To evaluate a series of drop-in workshops held at the Sojourner Truth Library during the Fall 1997 semester.
- To analyze data collected from questionnaires completed by participants.
- To interview librarians, administration, and support staff involved.
- To question administrators concerning an institutional commitment to information literacy.
- To appraise the effectiveness of such sessions in an academic library, when compared with a mandatory credit bearing course.
- To define the goals and objectives of bibliographic instruction at New Paltz, and to assess its place in a college wide information literacy program.
- To propose possible models for a college wide information literacy program at New Paltz.

RESEARCH QUESTIONS

In a study of data collected following the Super Searching Sessions at SUNY New Paltz, the researcher asks if the objective of getting students to attend optional drop-in classes is a viable means of library instruction? Can workshops, such as these, be an effective method of teaching research skills? Do they have a place in the library's user education program and/or in a college-wide information literacy effort? What is the administration's view regarding library instruction and a program of information literacy? How would librarians be involved in such a program? What steps are being taken to start such a program?

REVIEW OF THE LITERATURE

- ERIC. "Bibliographic education" listed under thesaurus term "library education" and "academic libraries." Searched under "information literacy" and "workshops" and "user education"; also under "library education" and administration and colleges. Searched under "lifelong learning" and "library instruction."
- LISA. Searched under "bibliographic instruction" and "academic libraries" and "information literacy" and colleges and administration.
- Dissertation Abstracts Online. Searched under "bibliographic instruction" and colleges and "information literacy."
- SearchBank. Searched under "Bibliographic instruction" and universities and "information literacy" and libraries. Also under the library and "undergraduate education."
- ProQuest Direct. Searched under "bibliographic instruction" and "libraries."
- DYNIX online catalog at Sojourner Truth Library, SUNY New Paltz. Searched under "bibliographic instruction–methods."
- Class readings from ISP 666. User Education. Instructor: Trudi Jacobson.
- FirstSearch. Searched the Library Literature database under "bibliographic instruction" and "academic libraries." Searched under "bibliographic instruction" and methodology.

METHODOLOGY

The researcher interviewed seven participants who were directly or indirectly involved in the creation and implementation of the Super

Searching Sessions. Data from student surveys were sorted and tables were created to display the findings. A sample survey form is in the appendix, along with curriculum materials from two of the sessions. Examples of marketing efforts for the sessions are also included in the appendix, as well as a strategic plan for an institutional commitment to Information Literacy developed by the Teaching Learning Technology Roundtable.

Library lectures were the earliest forms of bibliographic instruction. Scholar librarians were the instructors of these sessions, which began at Harvard, and later on at schools like Indiana University and Columbia. Oberlin College and the University of Michigan developed separate courses in BI in the late 1800's, but "by 1900, six of the seventeen institutions examined were no longer providing library instruction, and by 1903, instruction had been dropped by two more institutions" (Tiefel 318). In 1912, William Warner Bishop and William Fredrick Poole sought to make students independent learners; not far removed from today's "lifelong learners." Academic libraries were increasing in number and the concern for user education was revived. Between the latter years of the nineteenth century and the beginning of the twentieth, the focus shifted from "teaching the use of materials for research to instruction in access procedures" (Tiefel 320). This approach declined in the early 1900's, as basic reading, writing, and mathematical skills were needed for an industrialized workforce (Warmkessel 81).

In the 1960's Patricia Knapp was the first to introduce the concept of problem solving to library instruction. This approach, along with access-skills instruction, was to influence BI all the way through the 70's, until its merger with "concept-oriented instruction in the 1980's" (Hopkins 196). Perhaps due to the ideology of social service, teaching librarians felt obligated to not only provide access, but to assist patrons in the use of the various library search tools. BI became more complicated in the 90's, with the decline of a "generalist" education. The broad problem-solving approach to instruction was not viable in helping an undergraduate student to evaluate materials in terms of bias or discrepancies (Hopkins 198). Because of increased specialization, the role of the librarian instructor is more important than ever before. Students are confronted with the "truth" of a given discipline on a daily basis, and need to be able to evaluate the materials they find. Knowing about the structure of information and the different ways in which students learn, today's BI librarian has the opportunity to provide them with the critical thinking skills they will need for their future.

As recently as 1994, the Reference Department at New Paltz, had, in addition to its online catalog, a series of dedicated terminals, such as Expanded Academic Index, ERIC and PsycLit on CD-ROM. (Some of these computers were actually owned by the company and used by the library). There were also two subscription online stations, that provided document delivery when Mars was in Venus, with Mercury rising. In 1995, the library's own local area network was installed, with multiple licensing for its most popular CD-ROMs. A few techno-savvy students searched the Internet via Mosaic. Then along came Netscape, and everyone wanted to get wired.

By 1996, the Reference Department at New Paltz boasted a total of 19 public PC's for searching, not counting the OPAC. Electronic data-bases rapidly replaced CD-ROM's in 1996; the LAN was reduced to four stations instead of 10, and consortium membership provided the library enough clout to subscribe to pricey online databases, with full-text capability.

With so much new technology, Library Director Chui-chun Lee was concerned about the number of students being reached via the course-related sessions scheduled by faculty. She asked the Information Resource & Delivery Team (Reference Department), lead by Wilma Schmidt, to come up with a plan for expanding upon the usual course-integrated sessions. Perhaps they might try teaching students BEFORE the time of need. Lucille Brown, Kathleen Gundrum, Barbara Petruzzelli, and Wilma Schmidt were members of a task force to develop this plan for the Fall 1997 semester.

Many concerns had to be addressed: space for an electronic environment, to say nothing of technical considerations such as PC's, a projector, an instructor's workstation. What were the goals and objectives of this project, and how could these be carried out in a timely manner? The librarians chose workshops as a type of instruction that might be helpful for those students whose instructors never arranged for the usual course-related class. They also believed that some faculty members might recommend the sessions for research-related assignments. In a paper delivered at the twentieth National LOEX Library Instruction Conference in 1992, Mary Reichel said that college faculty projected that librarians would be teaching more workshops and short courses for students and faculty alike, especially in the area of electronic information. She further stated the importance of research in the area of information use for library instruction librarians, as a means of self-empowerment (Reichel 25). This was also an opportunity to experiment with an experiential element to reinforce learning.

The librarians agreed on four basic areas to cover–ERIC, the DYNIX online catalog, the SearchBank online database and the Internet. Each session would last 1 1/4 hours and be offered on a first-come, first-serve basis at various times during the semester. Plans began to gel, and a temporary space was found. The ensuing experiment was expensive, and raised the issue of how much should be spent to reach a small number of patrons. The greatest concern seemed to be how to get students to participate prior to their point-of-need.

The idea for the workshops came out of a day-long retreat for BI librarians in January, 1997. Barbara Petruzzelli notes that discussion centered around patron requests for help with some of the newer electronic resources. Petruzzelli was responsible for marketing the sessions: "From the beginning, hands-on was the most important factor. We knew we were not serving everyone with the old format, of a one-time, cover-it-all, course-related class. People need an interactive experience, in order to truly learn how to use a database or the OPAC. The key thing we need to remember is that we are not teaching our patrons to be librarians: we are professionals whose job it is to make information accessible to the people who need it" (Petruzzelli 7 July).

To develop a rapport with the user and to determine necessary concepts and skills, Petruzzelli is currently planning a collaborative effort with a faculty member, in which she will make additional classroom visits to reinforce concepts. Ted Clark, the instructor, said of past sessions with Petruzzelli, "They were great, but too much for the class. I already knew what the resources were and I was excited and eager to have my students learn about them but they were overwhelmed. I never thought about it from the student's point of view" (Petruzzelli 7 July).

With encouragement from Library Director Chui-chun Lee and William Vasse, the Vice President for Academic Affairs, a "temporary" electronic classroom was designated, in a small ($12' \times 20'$) conference room, located on the basement level of the library. Not only was expense an issue, but also the logistics of the configuration of eight PC's, plus an instructor's workstation. With a maximum of two participants per computer, the room could just about accommodate 16 students and a librarian instructor.

Sessions ran from October through December, each workshop being offered at different times each day, in order to provide maximum convenience for students and faculty. Out of a total of 18 sessions which potentially could have reached a maximum of 288 patrons, there were only 67 participants. Was the low enrollment a result of a naive notion that people might actually want to prepare for research AHEAD of time? Was it as low as all that? Must every course be for credit or course-related? Does such an effort have a place in today's academic library?

Success stories at other institutions involve a partnership between the library and a university wide goal towards "information literacy." While the term may be overused, the intent is to provide students with the survival skills they are going to need in the outside world. Virginia Tiefel writes in her 1995 Library Trends article about the Ohio State University Gateway project, that it "prepares people to use information effectively in any situation" (Tiefel 326). If technology has the capacity to process billions of units of information per minute and human beings can process only 300 units of information per minute, the ultimate goal must be to focus on access to the specific information desired. Because of ease of access at home, users today expect the same from the library: it is incumbent upon libraries to provide that convenience in a user friendly interface. "Today's youth, raised on computers, want a 'magic machine' which puts all the information they need for their assignments together for them at the touch of a button" (Murdock 27). This approach takes the term "user-friendly" to the extreme. In *Liberal Anxieties and Liberal Education*, Alan Ryan expresses the belief that today's liberal arts students "could be made to work harder," but the Ohio State model strives to make the research process painless for the student (Glazer 7). The direction of new and powerful database systems is to make research easier for the user. New search engines will include enhancements such as: "Beyond Boolean natural language querying and processing; integration of multiple techniques from fields of information retrieval, cognitive science, and artificial intelligence; systems that suit the style of today's nonprofessional Web-based user; and intelligent agents with improved filtering and profile technologies" (Kassler 74). Libraries can either offer the same kind of searching capabilities or be left in the dust, especially

when companies like Information Access Company begin to market their home products. The OSU Gateway emphasizes ease of access for the end-user, with self-help instructions for the student. Based upon the premise that users prefer computer assisted or one-on-one instruction, the system provides short narrative modules that allow the user to learn on his/her own. At the first screen the user is given just two choices: *subject* or *title*. Clicking on the subject option leads to a search strategy diagram, which suggests that the user can maximize results by following the instructions in order, from the top of the pyramid (general information), to the bottom (more specific). The creators of this system soon realized that users will read only about two lines of instruction at a time. These instructions lead the user to the desired online source or to a library location for a print source. The narrative directs the student to the best source of information for the search topic. By being able to save each segment to a "notebook," the user has an individualized folder of information appropriate to the topic, and ultimately can progress through access and evaluation of full-text materials. The system has proven to be a strong substitute for real-life instruction sessions (Tiefel 334).

An information literacy program developed at California State University at San Marcos followed the goals and objectives of ACRL's Model Statement of Objectives for Academic Bibliographic Instruction. Separate goals, objectives and competencies were written for each area of study within the college. The program had full administrative support, and was a high-visibility project for college librarians. Librarians served on nearly every university-wide committee, and participated in pedagogical workshops offered to the faculty, making for a comfortable partnership, despite increased work loads for all concerned (Sonntag 335).

The University of Washington has adopted a "holistic" approach to information literacy, which features librarians as active partners in its UWired program. Again, the project has had full administrative support from the start, with program funding from vendor contributions, endowment funds, capital projects, and the Provost. UWired begins with the Freshmen Interest Group (FIG), which divides new students into groups which take a "thematically linked suite of courses during their first quarter on campus" (Williams 4). In 1994, three out of forty-five FIG groups were enrolled in a two-credit technology seminar which was taught by a librarian. By 1996 all sixty of the groups received an introduction to information technology and electronic communications (Williams 5). Evaluations showed that UWired students were "five times more likely to know how to evaluate World Wide Web information, used the Web twice as frequently, were able to describe specific ways this information would help them, and felt more comfortable using the Web to find information than non-UWired students (Williams 6). One of the most favorable outcomes of the UWired project is that faculty now view librarians as more service and training-centered, than collections-centered. Librarians have felt empowered by this interaction and by being able to redefine their roles within the institution (Williams 9).

The Farnsworth Middle School in the Guilderland Central School District, in Guilderland, New York, has developed a Unified Research Model for sixth and seventh graders that focuses on a "process approach to research." This system emphasizes teacher and librarian as partners who work with the students on a specific project. The Model takes the participants through the initial steps of planning and preparation, to research classes, during which the teacher and librarian guide the student through the research process. Even the evaluation of the projects involves the librarian as well as the teacher. While some of the steps are simpler than a college setting would be, the guidelines are excellent for some undergraduate courses (Unified Research Model).

As libraries begin to focus on access to information, rather than ownership, the librarian must become increasingly proactive. That means assuming more of a teaching role. "Teaching concepts has replaced teaching tools and library instruction has become information literacy and lifelong learning" (Tiefel 1). Timely access of desired text and images is increasingly the focus of the latest technological developments. In 1992, Miller wrote that, "without a commitment to teaching, librarians will not be successful with information literacy and that, as collection development wanes in importance and access waxes, the teaching library is the natural route to go" (Tiefel 10).

Lucille Brown recalls the beginnings of a formal bibliographic instruction program for New Paltz, when she attended a LOEX conference in 1975. That trip was confirmation of her own philosophy, was derived from the study of pioneers like Patricia Knapp and Evan Farber. Prior to that time, library instruction had consisted of an orientation tour of the library and its resources that was conducted by anyone who was available at the time.

Because of her work on a Political Science bibliography, a member of that department asked Brown to elaborate on its use for his class. That was the start of a program of course-related sessions for interested instructors. As the program gained more popularity the Admissions Office, the Equal Opportunity Program, and enthusiastic faculty members, requested that the library institute a one-credit Pass/Fail course in the use of the library and its resources. This was a six-year effort, during which the popularity of the program grew in scope and in complexity: in addition to teaching classes and working at the Reference Desk, each librarian privately mentored a couple of students. Burnout began to be a factor, and the number of classes was decreased from seven or eight sections per semester, to two. An "advanced" section was created at about the same time the number of basic classes was reduced (Brown 16 July). While it may seem paradoxical to create a new class at such a time, Susan Blandy contends that BI programs are in need of constant evaluation and re-invention: "Any program goes through a cycle of design, delivery, and decay, a cycle from identified need to enthusiastic response to boredom and burnout" (Blandy 426). At about the point librarians feel they have said it all and teachers feel they could teach the class themselves, it is time for a new approach. Although the "advanced" class lasted only one semester, it proved to be a turning point. In 1986, Brown and Chui-chun Lee (the current Library Director) received a research and creative awards grant to develop a program, utilizing "Computer Assisted Instruction." They looked at various innovative programs at other colleges and designed their own CAI program, "Explore the Truth: your guide to the Sojourner Truth Library," which was used on a trial basis by two English Composition I classes, "in the Color Lab using IBM PC's with color monitors and graphic boards" (Brown 1). Despite promotion within the library and attempts to excite faculty members, the CAI package failed, a victim of its own premature invention. Brown reluctantly admitted that "unless it gets into the mainstream of academia and is linked to learning skills or general education courses, it will not accomplish its short range goals of reaching a modest sampling of 100 inexperienced users" (Brown 2).

With online catalogs and the advent of CD-ROM's and online searching, BI at New Paltz resumed a healthy course-related, schedule of classes, reaching a high of 2,099 students in 1996/97. Technological advancements required new skills, in order to effectively access information, and Brown and company were there to teach them. The library began to offer courses specific to these tools, even offering classes at alternative sites on campus.

The format for the drop-in classes was developed to serve as a replacement for a one-credit course called *Information Mastery*, which was offered during the Fall 1996 semester. According to Wilma Schmidt, Team Leader for Information Resource & Delivery, "That was an experimental effort, taught to a single group of Honors students, for whom it was *optional*. Our objectives were compatible with most definitions of information literacy, but we felt that "information mastery" put a positive spin on a phrase that has a negative connotation. In our course outline, we stated our objectives to be:

1. To recognize when information is needed
2. To know how knowledge is organized
3. To know how to locate information
4. To know how to evaluate the accuracy, currency and relevance of information
5. To know how to use information effectively (appendix A).

Eleven students signed up. We covered the online catalog, LC subject headings, research strategies, indexing, computerized databases and the Internet. Students also had to create an annotated bibliography. Participating students were enthusiastic, but the following semester only two students signed up, so the course was abandoned" (Schmidt 6 July).

As the committee was trying to find a way to reach a greater number of students, outside the credit course format or standard curriculum-based single BI session, it explored the hands-on workshop arrangement. Schmidt spoke of teaching the use of library tools by incorporating basic information literacy skills. The interactive lab setting was new, and the developers felt it to be a superior venue to the generic one hour lecture session, especially when teaching electronic sources. "The only thing I had trouble understanding is why people wouldn't take advantage of the sessions, but I think the bottom line is that you need support from the faculty and the administration. The classes were encouraged by the administration, but a curriculum-integrated, credit-bearing course, with faculty participation says you're really committed" (Schmidt 6 July).

Schmidt prefers one-on-one, or at least small-group interaction. She believes the reference interview and step-by-step research is highly effective, but points out that it is a luxury which is not always possible to indulge. "I have always liked the Brandeis model, where trained paraprofessionals would answer basic questions, and refer more complicated searches to a librarian. Signs and user guides work to some extent, but people don't read signs, or maybe they don't understand them. (Last week a young man told me he thought the sign over our OPAC-*Online Catalog,* meant *America Online.*) . . . It really takes great interpretive skill to be a reference librarian, because some people don't know how to ask the right question. Of course, the Brandeis model has problems too. It is a kind of tiered service that leaves some people feeling cheated because they don't get their information from a librarian" (Schmidt 6 July).

Sessions were not repeated during the Spring 1998 semester, due to staff shortages and a heavy course-related class schedule. Another reason was the poor attendance, but Barbara Petruzzelli remains optimistic about the Super Searching Sessions: "I know we should give this format another chance . . . tweak it, and do it again. For instance, we didn't offer any sessions after 5:00 p.m. Times were completely random–we might examine that, and maybe try for more faculty involvement. Face-to-face contact works best, if you can manage it. That's how this whole thing with Ted Clark came about. So I definitely would try again" (Petruzzelli 7 July).

Petruzzelli's marketing efforts involved not only a letter to deans and department chairs, but also direct mailings to each faculty member in Business Administration and Education; an ad and an article in the student newspaper; a feature in the library newsletter; a mention on the library's web page; and extensive postering on campus (appendixes B and C). Both Schmidt and Petruzzelli feel strongly about faculty involvement and administrative support, and that if Information Literacy is an institutional goal, related courses cannot be optional.

Any imagined threat of obsolescence for reference librarians does not concern Petruzzelli: "You do your job as a professional, with the idea that we are here to make information accessible to people who need it. We have to learn to be clever and adapt: if statistics are down, we need to figure out better ways to count. There can be counters buried on our web page, and we have to start counting the number of times patrons access our online databases. The fact that less people are coming to the library should not be viewed as failure, because that is what we have been trying to achieve . . . greater access to information and services. With any new technology there is a natural evolution of products and the marketplace. There has been a role for us for centuries and I believe there will always be" (Petruzzelli 7 July).

Statistics of participants' grade levels indicate strongest motivation from graduate students, with 24 attendees, or 35% out of a total of 67. That group was followed by juniors and seniors, which comprised another third of the total, while only nine freshmen and sophomores attended.

TOTALS OF PARTICIPANTS BY GRADE LEVEL					
Freshman	Sophomore	Junior	Senior	Graduate	Faculty
6	3	10	13	24	4
ERIC Totals					
0	0	0	0	7	1
DYNIX Online Catalog Totals					
1	1	1	4	4	1
WWW Totals					
2	1	3	2	7	1
SearchBank Totals					
3	1	5	7	6	1

Similarly, 24 transfer students made up a third of the sessions' numbers, and adult and international students accounted for a substantial percentage. (Some students represented at least two of those categories, while a couple were "adult-international-transfer" students.)

TOTALS OF NON-TRADITIONAL PARTICIPANTS		
Transfer	Adult	International
24	13	12

Of students who attended the workshops, the overwhelming majority found them to have been of value in assisting with searching strategies. Most (43) learned about the sessions through signage in the library, which is an indication that these participants must have been library users prior to these classes.

PARTICIPANTS LEARNED OF WORKSHOPS BY:							
Sign in Library	Student	Prof/ T.A.	Sign on Campus	Other	SUNY HOME PAGE	LIBRARY HOME PAGE	LIBRARIAN
43	5	14	1	4	2	2	3

Kathleen Gundrum would have liked more in-class promotion from faculty and greater visibility for the sessions. She suggests that more students might have attended if they could have seen the classes actually being taught. Contrary, to most opinions, Gundrum sees optional attendance as a plus: "I think it is just really necessary for the students to see what they can get out of these workshops, and how it can directly relate to them doing their schoolwork better and faster. Drop-in workshops are good because you know they are there voluntarily." Currently serving as Membership Services Coordinator at SUNY OCLC in Albany, she was the New Paltz librarian who created the curriculum for the SearchBank and ERIC sessions for the workshops (Gundrum 27 July).

Anna Badillo was the only technical support person at the time of the Super Searching Sessions. She was the sole installer of hardware and software in the PC's and the person who moved them to the classroom. She ordered the cabling and hub for the network, and secured delivery on a Light Pro 220X projector within three days of the order (at $3500). Badillo also got permission from Silver Platter to install ERIC and PsycLit demo CD's onto the hard drive of the instructor's station, in addition to regular Internet access, etc. "I spent probably between 40 and 50 hours physically setting things up for the room . . . and, of course, you have to take into account that things don't always work the first time you try them. We moved pretty quickly, because the wiring was already in place from last year's credit course" (Badillo 8 July).

Mehri Parirokh writes that two factors are of key importance in the implementation of effective user education programs: "policies within the library and the overall policies within the academic institutions in regard to the education of independent learners" (Parirokh 3765). Library administrators must see the value in a dynamic user education program, and must convey that vision to the administration of the university itself. At the same time the library director must take a realistic approach in long-range planning. Expenses such as hiring extra librarians to assist with instruction; an electronic classroom; additional help at the reference desk ; increased clerical help in preparing additional handouts; and planning time for instructors all contribute to a program that can be viewed as a sort of "budget vacuum cleaner," without some notion of what the end result can be for the institution *(Sourcebook* 223).

Because of her concern that New Paltz students have core competencies in information literacy, the sessions were supported by Library
Director Chui-chun Lee. Lee feels strongly that libraries must explore
alternative instruction venues. In "Library User Education: examining
its past, projecting its future," Virginia Tiefel writes that "librarians
need to look for additional ways of reaching students. Course-related
instruction, workshops, and handouts are still viable means of teaching information-seeking skills" (Tiefel 324). While Lee believes that
every effort was made to market the searching sessions to the college
audience, she was disappointed with actual figures, and concurs that a
credit-bearing, or class-related course recommended by a faculty
member might attract more students. "The sessions were highly pro-
moted, but they were not required . . . maybe if students had to at least
sign up ahead of time it would make a difference" (Lee 7 July).

The Teaching Learning Technology Roundtable (TLTR), a college-
wide committee co-chaired by the library director, is dedicated to
addressing the university's policies and goals concerning computer
and information literacy. The group's strategic planning document
states as a major goal "that all New Paltz students have meaningful
encounters with information technology," and that TLTR will strive to
make the integration of information literacy into the curriculum a
primary concern. Among specific recommendations are: orientation
that includes introducing incoming students to basic library and computer skills; amending the Core General Education Academic Requirements to incorporate basic computer skills into Freshman Composition I, and basic information skills into Freshman Comp II. TLTR
further recommends that "academic departments be encouraged to
incorporate information literacy as it pertains to their specific disciplines"(appendix E). Librarians would have designated liaison roles
with faculty members, assisting particular disciplines with development of lesson plans and research-related assignments.

The TLTR document is in direct response to the Middle States
Association of Colleges and Schools publication, *Information Literacy,* "calling for a pedagogical shift to integrate information literacy
into curricula and to reinforce it at every point in the learning process"
(Schmidt 2). Hannelore Rader believes that librarians need to define
their roles at the forefront of teaching and learning process reforms as
they occur, according to the 1994 Middle States Standards for Accreditation: "It is essential to have an active and continuing program of

library orientation and instruction in accessing information, developed collaboratively and supported actively by faculty, librarians, academic deans, and other information providers" (Rader 277). Accordingly, the librarians at New Paltz will increase their efforts in the overall areas of providing students the opportunity to acquire skills in computer and information technology.

A Computer and Information Technology (CIT) Across the Curriculum requirement would be instituted within the General Education Program. These courses would be designed to incorporate the use of information and computer technology. Budgeting is a concern for the library: "To implement this proposal, the College should provide resources for equipment purchase and maintenance, support staff, and faculty development. Also, the College should provide resources for classroom support infrastructure compatible with increased use of learning technologies." In our interview, Lee stressed the necessity for increased library staff and resources, in order to implement these major changes. "Relationships are created by librarians serving on committees, or sitting in on departmental meetings, but there are 12 librarians and over 30 departments, plus committees. On the one hand, it is very good, but also it takes librarians away from other responsibilities. We really have to decide what our priority is here in the library. If our overall goal is to become a "learning library," there needs to be more intra-team cooperation in order for the library to play a major part in the TLTR proposal." Although there is cooperation, there is room for improvement. She mentioned that librarians who are preparing for a class often have to beg for assistance from non-teaching librarians in covering desk shifts.

Another important factor is to teach the faculty concepts related to the organization of information. Inroads have been made, with librarians instructing Teaching Assistants from the English and Psychology Departments, so that they, in turn, may better teach their students. It would be logical to offer more training to faculty, so that they might give more effective library-related assignments. It could also mean librarians teaching outside the library, and is that what the library wants?

William Vasse is in favor of librarians teaching faculty and working on committees with faculty, to help promote an information literacy program. As Vice President for Academic Affairs, he sees the need for students to "have a meaningful encounter" with technology at New

Paltz. The Middle States Report strongly suggests a need for improvement in the areas of computer and information literacy, and some course-related work in certain departments is already under way.

Vasse's overall plan for implementing Computer Literacy and Information Literacy programs at New Paltz is divided into three components:

1. What do all students need to know? Those skills would be the ones incorporated into English Comp and Modern World classes. They would cover basic skills; how to use a computer, how to search for information . . . no extra credit.
2. What do students in particular disciplines need to know? These might be modular classes of perhaps 1/2 credit each, related to individual disciplines. There used to be two additional credits required for graduation when there was a physical education requirement at New Paltz. I would propose re-instating those two credits, which students would be required to complete by taking a series of mini-courses related to specific disciplines.

When the interviewer suggested that perhaps more librarians might be needed to handle something of this magnitude, he said, "This isn't just about the library . . . librarians would teach certain classes, they might teach faculty to teach, but experts in the field, or professionals from the computer center would also teach. Let's take a department we all know and love–the Theater Department. There are programs a student can use to direct a play, and there are certainly programs for designing sets and even patterns for building costumes.

3. What would be good for students to know if opportunity and cost allow? This is the last area, and would involve more intensive involvement with technology. We have a good deal to do before we get to that point (Vasse 16 July).

The Middle States Association Commission on Higher Education has suggested that the library work with faculty to build literacy modules into their courses and be directly involved in a college wide information literacy effort by building into the curriculum "more complex searching skills as they [students] progress in their academic education" (Tiefel 326).

CONCLUSION

Three separate issues were addressed in this paper:

1. A series of "drop-in" library workshops
2. BI program at the library
3. The library and information literacy at New Paltz.

1. There are several conclusions to be drawn concerning the Super Searching Sessions and similar informal workshops:

- Specific assignments lead to action. Most students want to know what they need to do and when they need to have it done. If it is not related to class work, it is going to take a back seat.
- Faculty involvement is critical to the success of any library instruction program. If teachers place a value on searching skills as they relate to course work, they will convey that to their students. If the sessions are repeated, there must be a concerted effort to involve faculty.
- Attendance was low in relation to the total FTE of 5977 enrollment at New Paltz, but not when compared to the potential maximum of 288 participants.
- Faculty are used to one type of library education. It will require some additional effort to sell them on something new.
- Library public relations were enhanced by the workshops. There were newsletter, newspaper, and web page advertisements, radio commercials, and posters proclaiming: "Hate to do research? Get over it!" in numbers that could not be ignored.
- An interactive electronic classroom is up and running. This space has already been useful for sessions with Teaching Assistants, prior to library-related assignments.
- Enthusiasm runs high during the talking and planning stages, but often wanes when it is time to show up for that ERIC or Internet workshop. Its level of import is automatically lessened if attendance is not required, in conjunction with a specific class assignment; and offering sessions on a "drop-in" basis indicates a minimum level of importance.

2. With continuing changes in technology, the BI program must experiment to find new ways to help students and faculty learn.

- Students gain the most when faculty and librarians work together. Faculty control library use by the assignments they give. Librarians are generalists; faculty are subject specialists. Research needs change as access changes (Blandy 435).
- In a world where access is becoming increasingly important, Computer Aided Instruction can supplement personal instruction. More powerful information retrieval systems will make searching easier for the end user (Farber 436).
- Students need to feel they can approach a reference librarian.

3. Plans for a college-wide information literacy program.

- Librarians have an opportunity to be proactive. "Classroom faculty know *what* they want their students to achieve; librarians know *how* students are working towards this goal" (Petruzzelli).
- An information literacy effort needs support from the administration, the faculty, the library and the computing staff.
- Librarians can be of tremendous assistance to faculty members who want to integrate core information literacy competencies into their courses (Oberman 347).

What is a realistic starting place for a campus-wide information literacy campaign? Time, resources and willing participants will tell the tale. With a variety of separate committees and coalitions working on the same issue, there has to be a common initiative. All of these individual groups must operate together towards the common goal as stated by the Middle States Association of Colleges and Schools: " . . . the need for a campus-wide commitment to information literacy as a strategy that will improve the immediate learning experiences of each student in every discipline and one that will enhance the student's lifelong learning" (Middle States 1).

Computer and information literacy have a greater impact on some disciplines than others. Librarians, Business faculty and Computer Services staff have already committed to partnership in a three credit course called Business Decisions Support Systems. Starting during the Spring 1999 semester, the library will be responsible for five hours of classroom time for a single section of the class, that will increase to four sections the following Fall.

The library has added a Seven Step Guide to Research to its web page, a PowerPoint presentation that provides a tutorial for students.

With easy-to-follow instructions that lead the user through the research process, this guide might be expanded to link students to information in a manner similar to the Ohio State self-help model. It could be used by Teaching Assistants or instructors in introductory-level courses with a research component.

The creation of curricula that incorporate technology into each discipline is formidable. It will happen where administrators and faculty push for it. Fewer single credit courses might be created more easily than a greater number of 1/2 credit courses. A one credit course in Computer Literacy, taught by Computer Services professional staff, that might be adapted across disciplines, is one possibility. A one-credit course in Information Literacy, team-taught by librarians and faculty, might be feasible, although additional librarians would certainly be needed. The importance of faculty partnerships with librarians and computer professionals in such an endeavor cannot be overstated.

Students want easy, user friendly access to information: the search engine and database designers are working to give them what they want. What will users need to know that future algorithms cannot calculate? Many will probably be satisfied, but some will know to ask a reference librarian.

Vice President Vasse emphasizes the need for a team effort: "Our students need to have meaningful encounters with technology while they are at New Paltz. There is the opportunity for high visibility for the library, but you have to understand, this is not something I can make happen. This sort of program will prosper or not, mainly because of the wishes of the faculty. It requires the interaction of faculty, librarians, and professional staff." Then he leaned back in his chair and smiled: " . . . I do not believe in a bleak, bookless future. Personally, I cannot imagine libraries without traditional monographs. I think we will always have books, but the selection process may become more finely tuned, with even more elaborate criterion before a book is added to the permanent collection. Some disciplines, in which there is a rapid change of knowledge–like Nursing or Engineering, may not require a book collection at all . . . of course you lose the serendipity factor, since you cannot browse through an electronic journal. But I take comfort in the fact that . . . we will always want to curl up with Shakespeare" (Vasse 16 July).

WORKS CITED

Badillo, Anna. Personal Interview. 10 July 1998.

Blandy, Susan Griswold. "Keeping Library Instruction Alive." *Reference Librarian* 51/52 (1995): 425-447.

Brown, Lucille. Personal Interview. 16 July 1998.

Brown, Lucille. Annual Report. Sojourner Truth Library. SUNY New Paltz. 1987/1988: 1-7.

Eadie, Tom. "Immodest Proposals." *Library Journal* 115 (1992): 42-45.

Farber, Evan Ira. "Plus Ca Change . . . " *Library Trends* 44 (1995): 430-437.

Glazer, Nathan. "After the Culture Wars." *New York Times Book Review* 26 July 1998, sec. 7: 6 +.

Gundrum, Kathleen. Personal Interview. 27 July 1998.

Information Literacy. Lifelong Learning in the Middle States Region: A summary of two symposia. Philadelphia, Commission on Higher Education, Middle States Association of Colleges and Schools, 1995.

Kassler, Helene. "The Search Engines and Beyond Conference." *Information Today* 15 (1998): 26 +.

Lee, Chui-chun. Personal Interview. 15 July 1998.

Lee, Chui-chun and William Connors. "Planning for Information Mastery." *Periodic Review Report.* State University of New York at New Paltz (1996): 89-91.

Oberman, Cerise, Bonnie Gratch Lindauer, and Betsy Wildon. "Integrating Information Literacy into the Curriculum." *College and Research Library News* 59 (1998): 347-352.

Parirokh, Mehri. "University Libraries as Contributors to Independent Learning: A study with particular reference to user education in Australian Universities." *Dissertation Abstracts Online.* 58 (1997): 3765.

Petruzzelli, Barbara. Personal Interview. 7 July 1998.

Petruzzelli, Barbara and Wilma Schmidt. "The Learning Library and Information Literacy; curriculum integration, courses, and collaboration." Paper presented at SUNY FACT conference on Instructional Technologies, May 1998, SUNY Cortland, Cortland, New York.

Rader, Hannelore B. "Information Literacy and the Undergraduate Curriculum." *Library Trends* 44 (1995): 270-277.

Reichel, Mary. "Information Use and Projections: The importance for library instruction (and Dr. Seuss)." Paper presented at Twentieth National LOEX Library Instruction Conference, May 1992, Eastern Michigan University. Ann Arbor: Peirian Press, 1993.

Schmidt, Wilma. Personal Interview. 6 July 1998.

Schmidt, Wilma. "Information Mastery Course Outline." SUNY New Paltz 1996.

Shakespeare, William. "Sonnet 18." *The Sonnets.* Ed. Douglas Bush. Baltimore: Penguin Books, 1972. 38.

Sonntag, Gabriela and Donna M. Ohr. "The Development of a Lower-Division, General Education, Course-Integrated Information Literacy Program." *College and Research Libraries* 57 (1996): 331-338.

Sourcebook for Bibliographic Instruction. Ed. Katherine Branch. Chicago: Bibliographic Instruction Section, Association of College and Research Libraries, 1993.

Steiner, George. "Ex Libris." *New Yorker.* (1997): 117-120.

Tiefel, Virginia. "Library User Education: Examining its past, projecting its future." *Library Trends* 44 (1995): 318-337.

"Unified Research Model: A process approach to research." Farnsworth Middle School, Guilderland Central School District, Guilderland, New York. 1996.

Vasse, William. Personal Interview. 16 July 1998.

Warmkessel, Marjorie M. and Joseph M. McCade. "Integrating Information Literacy into the Curriculum." *Research Strategies* 15 (1997): 80-88.

Williams, Helene and Anne Zald. "Redefining Roles: Librarians as partners in information literacy education." *2nd International Symposium on Networked Learner Support*, June 1992, Sheffield, England.

Guidelines for Creating
a Self-Directed Training Program
for the New Reference Librarian:
A Framework and Checklist of Activities

Jody Condit Fagan

SUMMARY. Although surveys of entry-level reference librarians have revealed that holding a Master of Library Science degree does not guarantee instant success at the reference desk, a majority of academic libraries do not have formal training programs. This article describes a framework for designing a self-directed training program for the entry-level reference librarian and lists examples of goals and activities to include in such a program. Hopefully, supervisors will continue formal orientation and training efforts and support and encourage self-directed long-term training as well. *[Article copies available for a fee from The Haworth Document Delivery Service: 1-800-342-9678. E-mail address: <getinfo@ haworthpressinc.com> Website: <http://www.haworthpressinc.com>]*

KEYWORDS. Reference training, self-directed learning, training programs

INTRODUCTION

In a 1996 survey of academic libraries conducted by the Association of College and Research Libraries, the majority of academic

Jody Condit Fagan is Assistant Social Studies Librarian, Morris Library, Southern Illinois University Carbondale, Carbondale, IL 62901 (E-mail: jfagan@lib.siu.edu).

[Haworth co-indexing entry note]: "Guidelines for Creating a Self-Directed Training Program for the New Reference Librarian: A Framework and Checklist of Activities." Fagan, Jody Condit. Co-published simultaneously in *The Reference Librarian* (The Haworth Information Press, an imprint of The Haworth Press, Inc.) No. 71, 2000, pp. 59-70; and: *New Technologies and Reference Services* (ed: Bill Katz) The Haworth Information Press, an imprint of The Haworth Press, Inc., 2000, pp. 59-70. Single or multiple copies of this article are available for a fee from The Haworth Document Delivery Service [1-800-342-9678, 9:00 a.m. - 5:00 p.m. (EST). E-mail address: getinfo@haworthpressinc.com].

libraries (57%) indicated they did not have a training program for newly hired reference librarians.[1] Of those with such a program, 84% of the respondents said their training needed improvement. Earlier studies by Karen Stabler and Heather Blenkinsopp on reference training activities found that although reference librarians received some basic orientation, such as tours of the library and reference department, descriptions of the job and the university, and basic computer training, interactive training (e.g., guidance on the reference interview) was provided to less than a quarter of reference librarians.[2] Yet in Ruth Bauner's survey of supervisors concerning abilities most needed in in-service education, knowledge of reference interview techniques ranked first.[3] The reasons for the lack of more formal training programs in libraries include a lack of priority, underfunding, limited personnel, and high turnover rates.[4] Recent graduates of library school may have been well-educated in the theories of library school and have a knowledge of basic reference sources, but "none will arrive as full blown searchers."[5] As Heather Blenkinsopp wrote, "those being trained in the provision of reference service are seeking more structure, better written guidelines, and a more inclusive program of reference training. What most are receiving now is spotty at best, non-existent at worst."[6]

Library literature contains some training and orientation checklists[7] that may be useful for supervisors to adopt to address the basics, but the subject of how to create an overall long-term training program for a new reference librarian is not discussed. Introductions or even intensive courses in on line databases, library resources, and reference sections are easily forgotten without practice and experience. Long-term training is necessary to build a broader experience base at an accelerated rate. Although mentoring by senior colleagues can fulfill a variety of training needs, juggling other work responsibilities make it difficult to make a comprehensive effort in this way alone.[8]

Self-directed training is a good option because it places a minimal burden on other staff, tailors training to the needs of an individual, and develops beginning library and instruction skills in the process. Although several different definitions for self-directed training have been proposed, all of them contain the ideas put forth by Stone in her definition:

In self-directed learning, individuals initiate and select their experiences and the other individuals who are to help them . . . Broadly defined, it means that the individual learner takes the initiative and responsibility to identify and assess learning needs, set goals, select and organize learning activities, and evaluate outcomes . . . learners take the initiative in making use of resources, rather than simply reacting to delivery from other resources. Self-directed learning implies and involves planned and intentional learning and this is different from random learning.[9]

This type of learning demands motivation, good planning, knowledge about available resources and how to find additional resources, and instructional development skills. Entry-level librarians have been introduced to these skills during their education and are likely to possess the initiative to develop them further. This article outlines a framework and activities for a long-term, self-directed training plan for the entry-level reference librarian.

A FRAMEWORK FOR TRAINING PROGRAM DEVELOPMENT

A myriad of books exists on developing training programs, should a new librarian not know where to begin.[10] The ACRL and the Association of Research Libraries have also collected and reported samples of other libraries' training and development documents, which may be helpful.[11]

The training plan should be discussed and agreed upon with the supervisor. Of particular importance is the degree of support the library will offer in the way of time and resources, and what opportunities exist for the librarian to seek guidance, for example, through mentoring programs or training classes. The supervisor and the librarian should plan a self-directed program that complements any existing training programs. Determining a training period timeframe is crucial for the librarian to plan her goals appropriately. He/she will need to consider how much time achieving each goal will take, and arrange a balance between training activities and other duties and responsibilities with the supervisor.

Based on the literature cited above, steps for creating the framework of a self-directed training program are outlined below. The last section lists possible goals and activities to fit into the framework.

CONDUCT A NEEDS ASSESSMENT

The new librarian should assess what he/she does not know about the community, the library, the collection, the patrons, and particularly his/her own job (e.g., tenure-track librarians need to find out promotion and tenure procedures). Consideration should be given to the policies, procedures, and philosophy of the library and the library's relationships with patrons and the community. Tougher aspects of needs assessment may include experiences that are not directly tested, such as the reference interview, collection development, and teaching skills. To gauge his/her skill level in these areas, the new librarian may wish to observe or interview senior colleagues about these activities, survey relevant literature, or participate in a reference listserv.

IDENTIFY OBJECTIVES

Upon outlining what areas of training are needed, the new librarian should formulate corresponding objectives, defined by Robert Mager as a "description of a performance you want learners [yourself] to be able to exhibit before you consider them competent."[12] Examples of potential objectives are given in the next section. The new librarian may worry at this point that the list of objectives shows incompetence. However, even experienced librarians would have a similar list of objectives considering the continual change of resources and technologies.[13] The librarian with a statement of goals for a self-directed training program will be ahead of 92% of the academic libraries with training programs, who, according to the ACRL, have no written program goals.[14]

COLLECT INFORMATION AND MATERIALS

To meet the prepared objectives, the librarian will need to develop a resource list. This list should include local materials about the collection, the library, and the community, as well as appropriate library literature. Reviewing some of her class readings and their cited references from library school would be a start. The librarian may need to solicit her supervisor's help to identify colleagues who are willing to serve as mentors and those who have relevant subject expertise.

DEVELOP CONTENT, PRACTICE, AND APPLICATION ACTIVITIES

In addition to reading and conversing with colleagues, the librarian will have to prepare some practical activities to fulfil her objectives. Some examples might be having senior librarians ask stumper questions, revising subject guides, or role-playing reference interviews. For some of these activities, it might be appropriate to involve staff members who might need some continuing education.

ASSESS AND REVIEW LEARNING

Assessment of the individualized training program may take different forms. The librarian may wish to submit a report to her supervisor summarizing her activities and the accomplishment of her objectives, particularly if she produced staff handbooks, subject guides, web pages, or similar materials. She may wish to keep a journal throughout her training time for her personal tracking. Seventy percent of libraries in the ACRL survey had no follow-up procedures to measure training program effectiveness–no wonder libraries have not realized the benefits!

POTENTIAL GOALS AND RELATED ACTIVITIES FOR A SELF-DIRECTED TRAINING PROGRAM

Below are some ideas for some goals a new librarian may want incorporate into a self-directed training program. For each goal, a list of possible activities is given. Rather than being an exhaustive list, it is an attempt to begin a brainstorm of ideas that could formulate a self-training plan.

Goal 1: Gain a broad understanding of library professional organizations with specific knowledge of professional opportunities in one's subject area:

- Solicit information from professional organizations on the national, regional, and state levels. Ask for bulletins and newsletters to find out what activities different organizations are involved in.
- Get information about local library groups, activities, and events.
- Find out which organizations have been valuable to co-workers, and what professional interests the other librarians have. Stay alert to those with similar interests to yours and ask to attend meetings with them.
- Find out what professional journals, if any, are circulated among library staff.

Goal 2: Understanding your library's organization, culture, and work practices:

- Ask for the organizational charts and mission statements of the college, library, and department.
- Learn the unofficial culture of the library by getting as many different perspectives as you can about library-wide issues, and watch to see how people work together.
- Solicit input from senior colleagues, who can help demonstrate the organizational and institutional culture of the library and the college or university.[15]
- After the initial library orientation tour, start making formal or informal appointments to meet with people to find out more about their work. Get to know support staff in other departments and how they work. There is plenty of practical knowledge that library schools don't (and won't) teach, but that staff have been practicing for years.
- Find out what other librarians' research interests are and look for collaborative opportunities.
- During the first few months, consider visiting co-workers in other divisions personally with questions rather than calling them on the phone.

- In group meetings, observe how the people relate to one another and try to discern communication patterns within your department and within the library.

Goal 3: Learn how your library practices collection development:

- Survey the literature regarding collection development theories
- Talk to co-workers in and out of your division who handle collection development. Discuss your findings in the literature with them to get a practical view of the theories you read about.
- If assigned a particular subject or subjects, visit the relevant departments on campus and meet the faculty during their office hours, perhaps with your supervisor or a colleague. Find out their perceptions of the library and what you can do for them. Be prepared to offer them any guides the library has on their subject area and offer avenues for future communication. Find out what research interests faculty in your department have.
- Examine the graduate and undergraduate college catalogs. Find out which programs have the highest and lowest enrollments.
- Visit the library's acquisitions department. Find out how they work and how you can make life easier for them. Trace the path of new books through cataloging, marking, and/or the bindery. Find out how long it takes materials to find their way through the maze.
- Consider having a sampling of the books you order sent to you as they arrive and evaluate some of your selections, particularly reference books.
- Read the book review sections of magazines and journals related to your subjects.

Goal 4: Get to know the university and community:

- Take a tour of campus, the kind given to prospective students. Feel free to ask the tour guide what her opinions are about the library, the safety of campus, and other topics. Try to learn the names of prominent buildings on campus.
- Read the local paper and find out how the university fits into the community.
- Look for literature on campus policies, news, and events.
- Read or skim through faculty, staff, and student handbooks.

- Take a class or ask a professor if you can drop in on a few classes.
- Get to know the major streets, landmarks, and libraries in the area.
- Visit the other libraries in the area, including public or school libraries. You may need to refer patrons to their collections.

Goal 5: Get to know the reference collection:

- When not scheduled on the reference desk, grab a subject guide or bibliography, and find out what the reference sources are good for.
- Discuss the creation or edition of library resource guides or subject bibliographies with your supervisor or senior co-workers.
- Make personal notes about resources as you get to know them.
- Study library guides, floor plans, collection strengths and weaknesses.
- Keep an eye out for ways to improve existing materials, practices, and collections.
- Volunteer to teach bibliographic instruction classes. It may take you much longer to prepare for a class than your co-workers, but you will learn more than your students in the process about library resources.

Goal 6: Become familiar with on-line resources:

- Get to know the on-line catalog. Ask the experts to show you the catalog's expert features. Consider visiting circulation, cataloging, and acquisitions to learn how they use the catalog.
- Get to know the campus and library web sites. Make notes about things you discover that are hard to find, and send the webmasters feedback.
- Ask your colleagues or supervisor to help you prioritize a list of electronic resources to learn. In a large academic library, learning how to use all the electronic databases with expertise may not be necessary.[16]

Goal 7: Developing reference interview skills:

- Consider having a colleague informally observe you at the desk and providing coaching-type feedback. Although new librarians may be initially intimidated, non-threatening methods such as Gers and Seward's peer coaching model can be used to alleviate fears.[17]

- Compare patrons' reactions to your style and that of your colleagues.
- Discuss when to refer a question with your supervisor. Consider "sharing" tough reference questions with senior colleagues.[18]
- Keep a lookout for ways you think reference service could be improved. When you try a new technique, consider writing a report or an article about your experiences.

Goal 8: Learn the customs of your reference desk:

- Some libraries may have training programs that feature direct reference training or a checklist of things to cover.[19] If your library doesn't have one, consider compiling one for future use.
- Get to know the etiquette of the reference desk. If there isn't a desk guide, write one, or revise an existing one to bring it up to date. Find out the mechanics of the desk schedule and if there are any meetings for reference staff.
- Find out if your department keeps reference statistics and how they are used.
- If e-mail or the telephone is used frequently for reference service, the new librarian may want to develop a training program for all staff, if one is not already available. Brian Quinn notes that telephone reference is often overlooked in library school courses.[20] Training sessions, quizzes, role playing, and coaching might all play a part.
- Read reference literature to stay abreast of the issues, particularly articles or books that discuss your subject specialty, if you have one. If you don't find articles or books on an aspect of reference service or your subject, consider writing one.

CONCLUSION

Many well-prepared surveys and reports about the training new reference librarians have been published, but libraries seem slow to support more formal training initiatives. Many librarians are stationed at the reference desk after only a few orientation activities, albeit amid helpful staff and co-workers. Constructing a self-directed training plan can provide more structure to the formless learn-as-you-go style that seems to prevail. With carefully formulated goals, activities, and evaluations, new librarians and their supervisors can have more confidence in the value of training. Although more libraries reported continuing education programs, perhaps self-directed learning could also play a role in refreshing experienced librarians. Hopefully, as new librarians importune their senior colleagues for help and wisdom regarding their new jobs, librarians will realize the need for all reference staff to participate in self-directed continuing education.[21]

TIPS FOR THE NEW REFERENCE LIBRARIAN

- Don't throw away anything from library school, especially notes and photocopied readings. As a new librarian, your memory will not be cued to the collection you are working in; it will be cued to the tiny (but solid) collection of library school notes and readings you have just worked with.
- The ready reference collection behind the desk can serve as an index for you to the regular reference collection. Use it to jog your memory.
- Use your unique position of having fresh eyes to your advantage. If you notice gaps in the collection or in library services, ask about them! If you can't find the appropriate resource, there are indubitably patrons who may also be struggling. Find out why you can't find what you're looking for–is it because you don't know? Or because there is something missing that could be easily provided?
- Find out how library technical staff do their jobs. They know lots of practical stuff that you probably weren't taught in library school. They know what TOGICed means.
- If you are or will be working at a library where librarians are tenure-track faculty, start writing research ideas down and fleshing them out now. Look through your student projects and reports, and see if there is anything that could be re-written for professional publication.

NOTES

1. Kimberley Robles and Neal Wyatt, compilers, *Reference Training in Academic Libraries* (Chicago: American Libraries Association, 1996), 4-12.

2. Heather Blenkinsopp, "How's the water? The Training of Reference Librarians," *The Reference Librarian* 38 (1992): 175-81; Karen Y. Stabler, "Introductory Training of Academic Reference Librarians: A Survey," *RQ* 26 (1987): 363-69.

3. Ruth Bauner, "Reference Ready beyond the M.L.S.," *The Reference Librarian* 30 (1990): 45-58.

4. Susan Jurow, "Preparing Academic and Research Library Staff for the 1990's and Beyond," in: *Developing Library Staff for the 21st Century,* ed. Maureen Sullivan (New York: The Haworth Press, Inc., 1992), 6; Mary M. Nofsinger and Angela S. Lee, "Beyond Orientation: The Roles of Senior Librarians in Training Entry-Level Reference Colleagues," *College and Research Libraries* 55 (1994): 162-66; Robles, 17.

5. Marilyn Miller, "What to Expect From Library School Graduates," *Information Technology and Libraries* 15 (1996): 45-7.

6. Blenkinsopp, 181.

7. Basic Reference Task Force, "Off to a Good Start: A Checklist for the Training of the New Reference Librarian," *Ohio Libraries* 3 (1990): 6-7; Berwind, Anne May, "Orientation for the Reference Desk," *RSR: Reference Services Review* 19 (Fall 1991): 51-54; Ruby A. Licona, "Planning Training Activities: A Checklist," in *The Tell it! Manual,* (Chicago: American Library Association, 1996), 50-9. Leonard Rhine and Trudi Di Trolio, "Using a Checklist for Library Staff Orientation and Training," *College and Research Libraries News* 11 (1992): 695; Robles, p. 27-28; Shelley L. Rogers, "Orientation for New Library Employees: A Checklist," *Library Administration and Management* 8 (1994): 213-217.

8. Nofsinger, 162-66.

9. Elizabeth Stone, "Toward a Learning Community," in *Continuing Education for the Library and Information Professions,* (Hamden, CT, The Shoe String Press, 1985), 54, 61.

10. Anne Grodzins Lipow and Deborah A. Carver, eds., *Staff Development: A Practical Guide* (Chicago: American Library Association, 1992); Peter R. Sheal, *How to Develop and Present Staff Training Courses, 2nd ed.,* (East Brunswick, N.J.: Nichols Publishing Company, 1994).

11. Kostas Messas, compiler, *Staff Training and Development* (Washington, DC: Association of Research Libraries, 1997); Robles, "Reference Training in Academic Libraries."

12. Robert Mager, as cited in Sheal, 81.

13. Murray S. Martin, "The Cost of Not Having Information," *Technicalities.* 16 (1996): 2-5; Anne Woodsworth, "Learning for a Lifetime," *Library Journal* 123 (1998): 62; Hunter Kevil, "Continuing Education and the Reinvention of the Library School," *Journal of Education for Library and Information Science* 37 (1996): 184-90; Jeanette Woodward, "Retraining the Profession, or, Over the Hill at 40," *American Libraries* 28 (1997): 32-4.

14. Robles, 4.

15. Nofsinger, 162-66.

16. Pat L. Ensor, "How Do I Keep Up on Everything in the New Electronic Information World?" *Technicalities* 16 (1996): 7-8.

17. Gers, Ralph, and Lillie J. Seward. "'I Heard You Say . . .' Peer Coaching for More Effective Reference Service," *The Reference Librarian* 22 (1988): 245-260.

18. Nofsinger, 161-70.

19. Basic Reference Task Force, 6-7; Licona, 50-9; Rhine, 695.

20. Brian Quinn, "Improving the Quality of Telephone Reference Service," *Reference Services Review,* 23, no. 4 (1995): 44-46.

21. Darlene E. Weingand, "Competence and the New Paradigm: Continuing Education of the Reference Staff," *Reference Librarian* 43 (1994): 173-182.

Outreach
Through the College Librarian Program
at Virginia Tech

Jane E. Schillie
Virginia E. Young
Susan A. Ariew
Ellen M. Krupar
Margaret C. Merrill

SUMMARY. Along with the capability of distributed computers, the University Libraries at Virginia Tech have invested in a program to distribute College Librarians into college buildings across the campus. Overcoming the disadvantages of a central library, the ten librarians allocated to six colleges perform outreach from offices among their constituents. This has allowed closer ties to faculty, resulting in more library instruction, more reference requests, and more placement of librarians on college committees and grants. Two evaluation surveys

Jane E. Schillie is College Librarian, College of Arts and Sciences, Social Sciences, Virginia E. Young is College Librarian, Human Resources, Susan A. Ariew is College Librarian, Education and Human Development, Ellen M. Krupar is College Librarian, Business, and Margaret C. Merrill is College Librarian, Agriculture, University Libraries, Virginia Tech, P.O. Box 90001, Blacksburg, VA 24062-9001 (E-mail: jschilli@vt.edu, gingery@vt.edu, saa@vt.edu, kellen@vt.edu, and mmerrill@vt.edu).

Address correspondence to: Virginia E. Young, Newman Library, Virginia Tech, P.O. Box 90001, Blacksburg, VA 24062-9001.

The authors are grateful for contributions to the article by their colleagues, Anita Haney, College Librarian for Arts and Sciences, Humanities, and Paul Metz, Principal Bibliographer.

[Haworth co-indexing entry note]: "Outreach Through the College Librarian Program at Virginia Tech." Schillie, Jane E. et al. Co-published simultaneously in *The Reference Librarian* (The Haworth Information Press, an imprint of The Haworth Press, Inc.) No. 71, 2000, pp. 71-78; and: *New Technologies and Reference Services* (ed: Bill Katz) The Haworth Information Press, an imprint of The Haworth Press, Inc., 2000, pp. 71-78. Single or multiple copies of this article are available for a fee from The Haworth Document Delivery Service [1-800-342-9678, 9:00 a.m. - 5:00 p.m. (EST). E-mail address: getinfo@haworthpressinc.com].

and an increase in outreach statistics have validated this four-year-old program. *[Article copies available for a fee from The Haworth Document Delivery Service: 1-800-342-9678. E-mail address: <getinfo@haworthpressinc.com> Website: <http://www.HaworthPress.com>]*

KEYWORDS. Outreach, college librarian, Virginia Tech

Between classes the student walks into the librarian's office to ask what database to use to find articles on cotton agriculture in depleted soils and the librarian demonstrates Internet access to *Agricola*. A professor walks in to ask how to use the high-price Internet database the library has just purchased, and the librarian walks to the faculty member's computer to demonstrate the product. Walking down the hallway to the water fountain, the librarian stops to greet a faculty member and discuss the semester's teaching assignment. Arrangements are made to schedule library instruction for a senior-level thesis course. These timely outreach scenarios are only possible because the librarian's office is not in the library, but where classes are taught and faculty offices are located–in the college buildings. This onsite outreach is the hallmark of the College Librarian program at Virginia Tech.

Over 85 percent of the University Libraries' collections are housed in Newman Library, allowing only three branch libraries, Art and Architecture, Geosciences, and Veterinary Medicine. While the economic advantage of centralized services has been important to the University Libraries, centralization often promulgates inappropriate "one size fits all" solutions to user needs. Along with the technological possibility of distributed computing power, however, comes the possibility of distributed librarian power. In 1994, the University Libraries launched the College Librarian Program, assigning subject and technology specialist librarians to offices in selected colleges. A physical location in the college itself becomes the ultimate tool in the library outreach program, creating a virtual branch library.

This "high tech, high touch" approach came when networked information resources were increasingly available, and with the expectation that librarians would be able to provide both publicity and instruction in their use. As described in earlier articles (Eustis et al., 1995, Stemmer and Tombarge, 1997), four librarians participated in the pilot project, serving the Colleges of Education, Human Resources, Agriculture, and Arts and Sciences. Close working relationships developed and College Librarians became integral players in the colleges' activities by virtue of their college offices.

Heightened awareness of the program resulted in requests from the nonparticipating colleges for librarians. In 1996, national searches added a business, an engineering, and a science librarian to the program. A reorganization in 1996-97 added collection development to the College Librarians' responsibilities, and allowed the reassignment of another librarian to the program. The faculty assigned to the College Librarian Program has grown from the original four assigned to the pilot project in 1994 to the current ten librarians. (The Virginia-Maryland Regional College of Veterinary Medicine and the School of Architecture retain traditional branch librarians, while the Geosciences Library houses the office of the College Librarian for the Arts and Sciences, Sciences.) Three librarians cover the College of Arts and Sciences, two are allocated the College of Engineering and the College of Human Resources and Education, and one librarian each serve the Colleges of Agriculture, Business and Forestry and Wildlife Resources.

Basic guidelines for outreach activities are outlined in the College Librarian's position description. Service to students, faculty and staff through traditional methods, such as one-on-one research assistance, group instruction, and collection development, is supplemented by posted office hours in the college office. While individual colleges consist of more than one building, College Librarians are generally housed in the main office building. There they find increased opportunities for meeting with faculty and students. These chance encounters often result in smaller, more detailed requests, but with bigger payoffs when completed.

Outreach statistics kept by College Librarians document the increased demand for their services, particularly library instruction sessions. During the 1995-96 academic year, four college librarians taught 3,559 students in 170 class sessions. The following academic year, eight college librarians taught 5,829 students in 273 class sessions, an increase of 60 percent.

College Librarians have been instrumental in keeping patrons informed of changes as new networked services become available, providing both software and instructional assistance. All venues of publicity are utilized, beginning with lunches with new faculty and continuing with messages sent to departmental listservs, brochures, announcements in departmental meetings, and by maintaining subject-specific web pages. In addition to links to electronic databases, full-text electronic resources, and selected Internet sites, the web pages contain contact information and provide a direct e-mail link to the College Librarian (http://www.lib.vt.edu/Resources/liaisons.html).

E-mail messages and web pages also serve as communication tools when announcing changes in library policies and services or when addressing problems that arise due to budget constraints. During several recent serials cancellations, web pages containing nominations for cancellation by title, fund code and call number were linked to the main library home page and allowed e-mail feedback to appropriate librarians. E-mail, phone calls and personal meetings assured timely communication with faculty.

A typical office in the college contains both pc- and Mac-based computers and printers, and sometimes a laptop for classroom presentations. The phone line is connected with voice mail, and there is a small collection of dictionaries, subject encyclopedias, and computer manuals. Specialized database software is available, as well as the office software used in the library. Located among faculty offices, and in a few cases in proximity to the college computer laboratory, the librarian's office is used for prior appointments or drop-ins during posted office hours.

While the College Librarian job description outlines basic guidelines for providing service, each college has different needs. Meeting these needs challenges the College Librarians to explore unique opportunities, to pursue creative projects and to form productive relationships with students and faculty. A list of examples of individual initiatives must begin with those of Susan Ariew, College Librarian for Education and Human Development, the quintessential College Librarian.

One of the original College Librarians, Ariew provides in her college office a collection of instructional software, and offers hands-on workshops in their use. Initial titles, purchased at the request of faculty and students, focused on methods for enhancing the curriculum. Ariew expanded the collection in 1997 with funding from Microsoft, received through her participation in the Instructional Technology Program. Recently, the College Outreach Program awarded Ariew

$250 to enrich the software collection after she conducted database workshops for school librarians.

Another collaboration, with the Human Nutrition and Foods Department, resulted in a $3000 Faculty Incentive Grant. Ariew provided software for preview and class use and helped create a web site, *Nutrition Central*, providing instructional information for children and nutrition educators (http://nutrition.central.vt.edu). In addition, Ariew has served on college task forces and committees including the Ad-Hoc Committee on Technology for K-12, and the Teacher Education Knowledge Group. She has also worked with faculty to develop new library instruction initiatives, distance education programs, and online course materials.

Joining Ariew as two colleges merged, Virginia Young, College Librarian for Human Resources, continues programs and instructional classes already in place. Young received a Virginia Tech ReachOUT grant of $5,750 in the spring of 1998 to develop a web site that disseminates information to help people lower their cholesterol (http://lowfat.lib.vt.edu). Faculty and students in the Department of Human Nutrition, Foods, and Exercise provide materials about exercise, food, and stress management and Young organizes the content, assists in html scripting and publicizes the site. The grant money allows her to hire a graphic design student, purchase low-fat cookbooks and other materials for review (and later donation to the library), and print bookmarks for publicity. This project demonstrates the close collaborative teams that can exist among faculty, students, librarians, and the hallmark of the land-grant institution, extension agents.

Extension agents are also a major component of the College of Agriculture, and Margaret Merrill, College Librarian for Agriculture, supports the mission of the Cooperative Extension Service and the Agricultural Experiment Stations by training personnel to access and use networked library services. The University Libraries' web pages address services for extended-campus students, faculty and extension agents, and Merrill uses these pages during hands-on classes or presentations at sites throughout the state of Virginia.

When asked to provide library instruction, College Librarians work with faculty to integrate information literacy skills into the course curriculum. The College Librarian for Business, Ellen Krupar, works with a marketing professor to design required instructional sessions for students enrolled in the Pamplin College of Business' basic marketing skills classes. Students learn how to formulate search strategies and navigate databases, receive an overview of *FirstSearch, Dow Jones,* and *Lexis-Nexis,* and are guided through an in-class assignment. That assignment and a homework assignment outside class account for 15 percent of a student's final grade. The collaborative relationship between Krupar and the marketing professor includes working together during class sessions to solve problems and taking time at semester's end for evaluation.

The outreach program has been active for four years and has been evaluated by a survey instrument twice. A preliminary survey was conducted in 1996, and in the spring of 1998 a survey instrument was distributed via e-mail to faculty. Nine questions addressed the issues of interaction, communication, office location, instruction, and assistance. Response rates varied by college and averaged a disappointing 12.5 percent. Of the 234 respondents, 85.5 percent said they had used the services of their College Librarian. Some conclusions about the program's effectiveness are drawn, at least from the perspective of those who were familiar with it.

Although it must be noted that the survey was conducted by e-mail, faculty overwhelmingly favored e-mail communication with their College Librarian rather than telephone calls or personal contacts: 82.8 percent stated they used e-mail to contact their College Librarian and 67 percent said they preferred their College Librarian used e-mail to communicate with them. Although the preference for electronic communication was strong, most respondents also favored having onsite librarians. Seventy-five percent thought the program's effectiveness was improved because the College Librarian had an office or held office hours in their College. The survey results from faculty who are housed in the same building as the College Librarian were even more significant–86.1 percent thought the college setting improved the program's effectiveness.

The survey results provided insight into the type of library instruction faculty deem beneficial. The respondents believe that their students need basic instruction in the use of the library. General instruction sessions, tours and discipline-oriented sessions were favored over assignment-oriented sessions, in contradiction to the views of librarians. Assignment-oriented instruction comprises the majority of classroom sessions the College Librarians teach.

Faculty voiced a preference for hands-on class sessions over lecture or demonstration and accordingly, the majority listed the library's computer classroom as their classroom of choice. With another 20 percent selecting another computer facility on campus as their preferred instructional setting, almost 90 percent of the respondents voiced their preference for a computer classroom.

When the College Librarian program first began, an emphasis was placed on providing technological assistance to faculty. Although 73.5 percent indicated they have asked their College Librarian for assistance in using technology, only 14.1 percent of the respondents ranked this assistance as the most important service provided. Instead, 59 percent rated reference assistance "of highest importance." While ratings varied by college, overall rankings indicated less valued services were identification of subject specific Internet resources, library instruction and collection development.

Evaluating the outreach efforts of the College is an ongoing process. Activity reports, submitted on a monthly basis, document the interactions between a College Librarian and members of his/her College and are used as a basis for performance evaluations. The activity reports also help the College Librarians assess their accomplishments and prove useful in identifying areas for future efforts.

Frequent and lively discussions among the College Librarians also provide a basis for assessing the program. As successful strategies and activities are shared, colleagues learn other ways to enhance the program and meet the needs of Virginia Tech's students and faculty. These discussions produce suggestions for communicating effectively with faculty, ideas for integrating information literacy skills into the curriculum and ways to meld traditional library materials with online resources.

Drawbacks of the program are also discussed. In a collegial spirit, College Librarians caution each other about the risks of "going native," a term they use to describe the conflicting loyalties and identities they sometimes feel when pulled in two directions. Reassigned librarians have developed a library culture from which they enter their college, but College Librarians hired by national searches must learn both the library and their college cultures. There is also the temptation to give collection development, or other library duties, lower priority in favor of college contacts.

Tension can arise between College Librarians and their colleagues in the Reference Department. There is still a need for functional specialists, such as an electronic resources librarian, a government documents librarian and others. These librarians also do the majority of reference desk hours, although College Librarians insist on keeping some desk hours believing that to be the best point of contact with undergraduates. Fulfilling duties and keeping offices in two places is difficult to do.

In response to very flexible job descriptions, the College Librarians at Virginia Tech have made great strides in several directions of outreach, while also pursuing collegial goals. Individually or collectively, the College Librarian program works to implement the Libraries' response to the "Implementation Plan of the Academic Agenda of Virginia Tech": "To create an atmosphere where learning can occur regardless of time or distance" (p. i). Though only four years in existence, the program might serve as a model for other large library systems seeking to achieve active outreach without the diseconomies of branch structures.

REFERENCES

Eustis, Joanne, Linda Maddux, and Dana Sally. (1995). "The Collegiate Librarian/ Information Officer Program at Virginia Tech," *Virginia Librarian*. 41, p. 13-16.
Office of the Senior Vice President and Provost. (1997). "Update to the University Plan: 1996-2001. The Implementation Plan," Virginia Tech, Blacksburg, Virginia. Typeset.
Stemmer, John K. and John Tombarge. (1997). "Building a Virtual Branch," *College and Research Libraries News*. 58, p. 244-248.

Choosing Between Print
and Electronic Resources:
The Selection Dilemma

Lou Ann Stewart

SUMMARY. The availability of resources in both print and electronic formats poses a selection dilemma for librarians dealing with rising costs of materials and stagnating or declining budgets. Should a choice between formats be made? There are readily identifiable differences between print and electronic resources and each has strengths and weaknesses. Traditional selection criteria are still valid for evaluating electronic resources but additional issues such as technology, access method, overlap between indexed publications and the library's collection, service implications, archival concerns and availability of new product information must be considered. Decision models can allow for easier comparison of information formats. A collection development

Lou Ann Stewart is affiliated with SUNY-Albany, Nelson A. Rockefeller College of Public Affairs and Policy, School of Information Science and Policy.

Address correspondence to: Lou Ann Stewart, 4 Jason Lane, Clifton Park, NY 12065.

[Haworth co-indexing entry note]: "Choosing Between Print and Electronic Resources: The Selection Dilemma." Stewart, Lou Ann. Co-published simultaneously in *The Reference Librarian* (The Haworth Information Press, an imprint of The Haworth Press, Inc.) No. 71, 2000, pp. 79-97; and: *New Technologies and Reference Services* (ed: Bill Katz) The Haworth Information Press, an imprint of The Haworth Press, Inc., 2000, pp. 79-97. Single or multiple copies of this article are available for a fee from The Haworth Document Delivery Service [1-800-342-9678, 9:00 a.m. - 5:00 p.m. (EST). E-mail address: getinfo@ haworthpressinc.com].

policy that incorporates electronic resources is a necessity that both justifies decisions made and ensures that resource collection supports the library's goals. Experiences shared by today's librarians illustrate the complexity of this selection dilemma and highlight the fact that there is no simple answer. *[Article copies available for a fee from The Haworth Document Delivery Service: 1-800-342-9678. E-mail address: <getinfo@haworthpressinc.com> Website: <http://www.HaworthPress.com>]*

KEYWORDS. Print and digital sources, evaluating digital sources, collection development

INTRODUCTION

A dilemma exists in libraries today. The cost of materials whether print or electronic are ever increasing while library budgets continue to stagnate or decline. Amid these economic pressures, librarians must make difficult decisions about how to best provide their users with the information they need. When that information is available in both print and electronic formats, how does the librarian make the choice between the two? Must a choice be made at all or are there circumstances that necessitate the availability of both resource formats in the library? This paper will focus on this selection dilemma and will examine: the differences between print and electronic resources, the advantages and disadvantages of both of these forms of information, criteria for and issues related to the selection of print and electronic materials, the impact on collection development policy statements, and experiences of librarians who have faced this selection dilemma.

DIFFERENCES BETWEEN PRINT AND ELECTRONIC RESOURCES

CD-ROM products, remote and networked databases, online services, electronic journals, Web-based products and the Internet are all electronic resources available to libraries today. There are inherent physical differences between electronic resources and their print counterparts. Although many of the differences are obvious, it is important to understand them before moving on to a discussion of why one format of a resource might be selected over another for inclusion in a library's collection.

Print resources are localized to a specific library. Unless multiple copies reside in the library, a print resource can only be read by one person at a time. Usually, print resources are relatively inexpensive, available to the reader at no charge, and require no special equipment to access the information contained within (Null cited in Pastine 1996). Often, a print resource can be described by its cover. Books and other print resources are tangible objects that are purchased. Their content is static. They arrive at a library in boxes to be unpacked (Kluegel 1997). Librarians often speak of ownership when referring to print resources and there is a certain amount of prestige that comes with that ownership. Academic libraries in particular "measure their greatness on volume counts" (Machovec 1990, p. 27).

By contrast, electronic resources can be available to many libraries at the same time and as such accessed by many people at once. Electronic resources are expensive and often carry a fee (Pastine 1996). Electronic resources are fluid by nature–their content can change without warning. They have no cover to speak of. Many are leased, not purchased. They arrive at a library through cables and modems (Kluegel 1997). Often, electronic products are offered in combination with other electronic resources and defining what is packaged together can be difficult. Access to resource A may require that the library also acquire resources B, C and D as well. Or, resource A may be available as both a CD-ROM product and a Web-based product but the content can vary widely (Schumacher 1998). Instead of ownership, librarians describe the possession of these resources in terms of access and use.

ADVANTAGES AND DISADVANTAGES OF EACH FORMAT

In choosing materials for a library's collection, the selector must be aware of these differences for the products under consideration. However, the mere fact that a product exists in both print and electronic format is hardly enough information on which to base a decision. Consideration must be given also to the advantages and disadvantages of each resource, their relative strengths and weaknesses.

There are several advantages to using an electronic resource over a print resource. The advantage most often cited is that electronic resources are easier to use since they usually offer some type of searching capability. Studies show that library patrons prefer using a CD-ROM database over a print index for several reasons, including speed, convenience, usability and completeness (Compton 1991 and Condic and Lepkowski 1994). One school librarian stated that using computer databases is advantageous for finding reference type statistics–"anything that is fast changing or short or accessed in small pieces, such as biographical sketches, encyclopedia articles, almanac entries, catalogs, quotations, poetry, laws, court decisions, chronologies . . . I appreciate the CD-ROM periodical index so much that I rarely touch the green books anymore" (Boardman 1996, p. 19). Electronic resources have the advantage of currency as they are updated more quickly and more often than their print counterparts. In addition, electronic resources occupy less space in the library facility. Reducing the number of print materials in favor of access to full-text databases could result in a decrease in library operating costs associated with ordering, cataloging, claiming, shelving and binding. Additionally, unlike print materials, "electronic articles cannot be mutilated, stolen or misshelved" (Hawbaker and Wagner 1996, p. 108). Electronic resources have the advantage of access because they can accommodate more people at a time, however, there are limitations. Restrictions may be placed on availability such that only those users in the immediate library community may have access to the information. This could be viewed as a disadvantage particularly by those outside the library community. A different view of access is that many research materials, such as old manuscripts, may only be preserved for generations to come through the use of technology–certainly an advantage over paper that deteriorates with age (Boardman 1996).

Print materials have the advantage of being immediately accessible and tangible provided they are not checked out, on loan, missing or misshelved. They have the advantage of the here and now and are not subject to the whims of technology. Much has been written about the ability of print material to allow for serendipity–certainly an advantage over electronic resources where browsing is difficult at best. Through the use of interlibrary loan, print materials may be shared with users who are not part of the immediate library community, again an advantage over the limited access restrictions of some electronic products. Other discussions on the advantages of print resources follow the thought that there is a heritage and a wealth (Boardman 1996) in a collection of books. "Books support the sustained development of ideas" and represent "the whole complex of knowledge" (Boardman 1996, p. 19). They represent "the record of humanity's struggle" and as such they are "an emblem of the culture" that created them (Campbell 1998, p. 263). Electronic resources enrich many subject areas but some argue that they do not provide the in-depth view of a subject that print materials do (Boardman 1996).

SELECTION CRITERIA, ISSUES AND DECISION MODELS

Traditionally, librarians have relied on a set of criteria by which to judge print materials. Most selection criteria for electronic resources have developed from this long-established list. However, the nature of electronic resources requires that these traditional selection criteria take on an added level of complexity and their complexity raises additional issues. For the librarian faced with choosing between electronic and print resources that deliver the same information the question that must be asked about the electronic product is: "Does it do more than can be done with print?" (Caywood 1996, p. 169). Or, conversely: What information is lost by choosing this electronic resource instead of the print material (LaGuardia and Bentley 1992)? Evaluating selection criteria can help answer these questions and decision models have been developed to aid in the selection and comparison of print and electronic resources.

The discussion will begin with a look at the traditional selection criteria and how they have broadened in scope to include electronic resources. This will be followed by an examination of additional selection issues and decision models.

Selection Criteria

The traditional selection criteria are well known and are designed to evaluate:

- the content of the material; its coverage, intended audience and quality, including the reliability, accuracy and currency of the information
- the source of the information; the authority of the author and publisher
- the cost of the resource
- the format or features that add value to the title.

The familiar questions asked of print materials may be asked of electronic materials but with a broadened scope.

Content

When considering the content of a print resource, it is a relatively straightforward decision based on a review of the item (Davis 1997). With electronic resources, it can be difficult to determine the actual material included in the product. A CD-ROM offering and a Web-based version of the same database may in fact include different journals or cover different time spans. Learning about these variations from the vendor can be frustrating and unrewarding as some are reluctant to share this information (Schumacher 1998). It is necessary to evaluate the quality and quantity of the data in an electronic resource which may include not only text but also images and often "audio or video components which should be seen or heard before a final decision is made" (Davis 1997, p. 394). Many selectors have come to rely on thirty-day trial copies of products to aid in their review. Some even take this a step further and volunteer the library as a beta test site for a new product. Many products are brought to the market quickly and as such are missing back files, contain only partial indexing (Davis 1997), or don't perform as expected, and often only a hands-on review of the product brings these problems to light. "Content is king" (Schumacher 1998) and quality can be a useful measure of content in comparing a print and electronic resource that does not need to be duplicated in a collection. One example given is that of a print encyclopedia and its CD-ROM counterpart. Although equivalent for most of the quality factors, the CD-ROM version fails when the issue of accuracy is addressed. The search capability does not function as expected because of misspellings in the text of the CD-ROM product. The print version has no misspellings in the text and thus is selected because of its perceived higher quality (Vogel 1996).

As mentioned earlier, some electronic resources are offered as part of a larger package so that the additional materials as well as the product of interest must be evaluated as to their suitability to the needs of the collection. Electronic resources alter access to information by allowing a user to navigate the material at will. As part of this expanded access, selectors must examine the quality of the interface to the desired product, its friendliness, ease of use, retrieval capabilities and response times. The audience's ease in scrolling through menus and entering commands is an important consideration. Particularly for Web resources, the electronic environment raises questions about the currency and reliability of the information presented. Selectors must consider the frequency of product or Web page updates as well as the stability and longevity of the information. In that environment, the content of links must be evaluated for their suitability for the intended audience.

Source

With traditional materials, the authority of the material, that is the reputation of authors, illustrators, editors, and publishers of a work is a major selection criterion. In the electronic environment, the idea of authority takes on a whole new meaning. All those involved in the creative process, including the author of the search software, the database designer and the home page developer, must be examined (Davis 1997). Internet resources that are developed by an academic institution or a government organization will have an established reputation in a subject area. A selector must also analyze the quality and quantity of technical and vendor support. Companies that provide an 800 number for customer service or that furnish monthly printed reports containing usage statistics of their product add value to their offering. As important as a vendor's track record is the perceived stability of the company. Having a sense of whether or not a vendor will still be in business next year greatly influences a decision. As a result, many librarians "rely on products from large producers/distributors, such as UMI, SilverPlatter, and EBSCO, not only for quality of content but also for the reliability of software, ease of access, and customer support . . . New partnerships of author/publisher and producer/distributor have become meaningful and worth examination in the selection process" (Davis 1997, p. 394).

Cost

Electronic resources are in most cases more expensive than their print counterparts. Pricing structures are complex. Selectors must be aware that some publishers offer significant discounts for access to their electronic product if the library continues with a subscription to the print version as well. There are other costs besides those associated with a particular product that must be evaluated with electronic resources. There are the costs incurred for the initial and continuing investments in equipment–hardware, software and wiring–necessary to access the resource. This requires reviewing the room available within the library facility and confronting any space management issues.

Librarians face financial risks when they commit large sums of money to a particular technology or software platform. The technology can become outdated quickly. The product can be replaced by an alternative, or the vendor can go out of business. "The total cost of a wrong decision can be intimidating" (Johnson 1996, p. 11). A local school librarian laments how the DOS-based products purchased three years ago had to be replaced with equivalent Windows versions at a loss of $3000. "Technology can bite you on the hand" (Ratzer 1998).

As part of analyzing the cost of an electronic resource, selectors must learn to evaluate not only pricing structures but license agreements and contracts. "In particular, the selector must examine issues of user definition, use rights and restrictions, and contractual obligations and penalties" (Davis 1997, p. 399). Defining the user of a resource was never a consideration with print materials, but because the pricing structure of electronic resources is often based on the number of users, librarians must give this their attention. Librarians must define all potential users who will access a particular product and then secure a rental contract or license agreement to allow such access. This includes understanding how the user community will access a product and assuring that such use is allowed by the license agreement. Often the terms of an agreement must be modified to the satisfaction of both the vendor and the library since many specify particular actions for which the library is held responsible. Selectors must understand that there are consequences to signing a rental contract or license agreement. An excellent Web resource, *Lib-license* (www. library.yale.edu/~llicense/warrels.shtml), assists librarians with the understanding of legal terms and licensing issues (Duranceau 1998). Librarians are not legal experts. They must know their institution's policies and understand who is qualified to sign these agreements (Miller 1998).

Format

One final set of traditional criteria that selectors depend upon is an item's format or special features. For print materials this might include the organization of the text, including the existence of features such as indexes and bibliographies, or the quality of the illustrations. As discussed earlier, there are many formats of electronic resources–CD-ROM databases, online database service providers and Web-based products to name a few. Specific considerations for database products include whether the format of the information provided is citation only, both indexing and abstracts, full-text, directory or multi-media. For Internet resources, an essential question is: Do all the parts work? Links and interactive portions should appear after the content, audience and essential instructions are outlined (Schumacher 1998).

When evaluating an electronic resource, the selector must also consider the network and format that comprise the library's electronic collection. A resource must be examined in terms of whether or not it is compatible with existing hardware and software. If a desired item is not compatible, "it simply should not be selected" (Davis 1997, p. 396). Special features such as documentation, user manuals and guides, and online help add value to a product. If applicable, the treatment of graphics and formulas is also important as is screen display and design.

Additional Selection Issues

In addition to these traditional selection criteria, the complexity of electronic resources raises additional issues that must be addressed. These include:

- technology in the library
- desired access method
- overlap between indexed publications and the library's collection
- service implications
- archival concerns
- availability of information about new products

Technology in the Library

There are specific hardware, software and telecommunications requirements that must be understood before selection of electronic resources can occur. There is often complex terminology to master such as Z39.50 compliance or graphical user interfaces (GUIs). Without understanding these and other terms, an informed decision cannot be made (Davis 1997). Electronic resources cannot be selected in a vacuum without the knowledge and support of the technical comput-ing staff of the organization. "Content may be king but bandwidth is queen" (Schumacher 1998). The tasks involved in the selection pro-cess should be divided between subject specialists and those with in-depth technical expertise. Decisions must be made in accordance with the technical goals and objectives of the institution.

Desired Access Method

Access to electronic resources can be achieved in several ways. Specifically, for commercial databases, the desired information can be acquired through a local CD-ROM network, via a direct connection to a vendor's computer that contains the desired data, or via a Web address maintained by the vendor that provides access to the data. Another option which carries many technical and support staff con-cerns is the ability of a library to purchase data directly from the vendor, load it into a local computer and run and maintain access to it independent of the vendor. There is a growing trend to access com-mercial database resources over the Web. Similar to the above discus-sion on technology issues, a selector cannot make a decision on access method without consulting other staff, particularly the technical sup-port staff, and without an understanding of the institution's future vision (Schumacher 1998). Access to Internet resources will be af-fected by the choice of Web browser used. Users will become easily frustrated if a particular site is difficult to reach either because it is overloaded or the Uniform Resource Locator (URL) changes.

Overlap Between Indexed Publications and the Library's Collection

Many electronic database products are indexing and abstracting ser-vices. If the library intends to provide access to this kind of resource, the question needs to be asked as to whether or not the library can also provide access to the texts which the user desires. If they are not part of the local collection will the user be able to gain access to them through interlibrary loan or a document delivery service? Consideration must be given as to how to provide material with a minimum of frustration for the user (Gupta 1993 and Martin and Rose 1996).

Service Implications

Acquisition of electronic resources impacts library services particu-larly in reference, bibliographic instruction and interlibrary loan. Some libraries have increased the number of staff at the reference desk to assist users with one-on-one searching as well as to answer questions on using equipment. In larger libraries offering many different databases, some with complex access, it is necessary to determine which staff members will be responsible for understanding the depth and breadth of the electronic collection and subsequently to develop a plan for staff training (Martin and Rose 1996).

Bibliographic instruction services are greatly affected by electronic resources. Questions are raised about the skills a user will need to access a product, how the user will be taught these skills, how much they will be taught and who will teach them. The level of end user training that the library is willing to provide has a direct bearing on staff job responsibilities. It is a difficult and time-consuming task to develop special workshops or seminars and to produce user guides and handouts. It can also be a major expense for a library because for this type of instruction to be most effective a library should have an electronic classroom (Martin and Rose 1996).

Interlibrary loan transactions can increase dramatically with the acquisition of electronic resources. As mentioned before, if the holdings of the library don't match the coverage of a database, users will rely on interlibrary loan or document delivery services to acquire the desired information. One rule of thumb to help alleviate this problem is, "If a library has only five to ten percent of the journals indexed in a database of considerable interest to its users, then it is probably not a good idea to subscribe to it" (Martin and Rose 1996, p. 99). However, if the user community continues to demand access to the materials it can be used as leverage to build the collection. Ultimately, access to full-text databases will be a long-term solution.

Archival Concerns

When considering whether an electronic product offers advantages to users over print, the selector must examine whether any information is lost if the print tool is replaced with an electronic product. Many electronic databases maintain only a limited amount of archived information in machine readable form and some vendors are not explicit about the contents of their files. A company that assures access to the last five years of a publication may adopt a "rolling-off theory" where with each yearly update the last five years *only* are available (LaGuardia and Bentley 1992). A user in need of a complete search may require access to print sources. If the library has made the decision to cancel the print subscription there are now concerns about the ease with which a backfile of the printed source can be found.

The archiving of electronic resources raises security concerns of a different nature than those related to print materials. There are questions related to the security of data files and operating software. If electronic resources are to circulate, there is the threat of computer viruses. The selector must work with technical staff to be assured that there are mechanisms in place to handle anticipated problems.

There are also doubts about the long-term preservation of electronic resources, in particular, CD-ROMs. Their longevity is dependent on the quality of the material with which they are coated and the cleanliness of the conditions during manufacturing. "Little is actually known about the physical durability of compact discs" (Condic and Lepkowski 1994, p. 49) and if they are not handled properly they will deteriorate quickly.

Availability of Information About New Products

Similar to traditional selection criteria, sources of review material about print resources are well-known and long-established. By contrast, the world of electronic resources has been described as unruly at best, and keeping abreast of changes and new products is a challenge for selectors.

Often the only way to gain information about a product is to see a demonstration at a conference (Johnson 1996). Traditional review literature does cover CD-ROM products, online access to full-text databases, electronic journals and Web sites, but selectors must also consult catalogs, publication announcements, colleagues, electronic listservs, and reviewing sources on the Internet. The most recent issue of *Choice* (October 1998) illustrates the changes taking place. An advertisement for *Literature Online* from Chadwyck-Healey–"Home of the Humanities on the Web" promises Internet access to over 350,000 full texts of classical and contemporary literature works. Interested parties are invited to try a 30-day complimentary preview at testdrive.chadwyck.com (*Choice,* p. 271). Even *Choice* itself is undergoing a change. Beginning in January 1999 *Choice* offers a Web-based review service that contains reviews from 1988 to the present. Customized notification of new reviews will be available to users along with other special features (*Choice,* p. 305).

Selection Models

There are strategies and models in the collection development literature that are available to assist in the selection and comparison of resources available in print and electronic formats. The models are presented in one of two formats: text-based or matrix-based. The first approach, text-based, presents the selector with a set of questions to answer regarding a particular product (Johnson 1996). The questions must be answered repeatedly for each product under consideration. Then, the selector must compare the responses to determine which information resource is appropriate for the library. The second model, matrix-based, includes both selection criteria and the format of the information resource in its framework. Space is provided for comments regarding each unique feature being considered. This strategy allows for easier comparison (Aston 1996). Some models go a step further and separate evaluation criteria and cost criteria into two separate matrices (Johnson 1996). As with any general model, each must be modified to reflect any special considerations of the library selecting the resources in question. While these models seem simple to the point of being trivial, they are valuable for assisting selectors in gathering their thoughts and information about the complexities of a resource in one place. The matrix-based model seems like the easiest and most comprehensive method to compare resources.

IMPACT ON COLLECTION DEVELOPMENT POLICY STATEMENTS

A collection development policy statement, as stated by the ALA, defines a library's existing collection, details the relationship between a library's priorities and goals and its selection criteria, and outlines a library's plans for future collection development (ALA 1987 and White and Crawford 1997). The question has been raised often as to whether or not collection development policies are still relevant in today's technologically oriented libraries (White and Crawford 1997). Past studies (as referenced in LaGuardia and Bentley 1992) have shown a reluctance to develop written policies for electronic resources. A survey of ARL libraries conducted in 1990 showed that only 18 of 73 had written selection criteria for electronic resources. A similar study conducted by the ALA in 1989-90 found that only 3 of

44 libraries that provided locally mounted databases had a formal collection development policy and 35 had no policy and no plans to develop one. However, more current literature on the subject indicates overwhelmingly that some kind of policy statement is needed that outlines specific selection criteria and addresses the issue of what information is lost by replacing print materials with electronic products. The selection of resources without the guidance of a collection development policy creates chaos, a sense of a lack of direction and "haphazard unfocused groupings of resources that may or may not support the mission of the library" (Vogel 1996, p. 65).

There is disagreement, however, as to whether there should be one comprehensive collection development policy statement for an institution or separate statements for different information resource formats (LaGuardia and Bentley 1992). There are, arguably, advantages to incorporating electronic resources into a comprehensive policy statement. First, by including all information resources into one statement, librarians can more easily compare materials that are in the same format and across formats and thus more easily recognize unnecessary duplication and gaps in a collection. "A librarian may realize that the library now owns a print resource and electronic resource that are nearly identical (e.g., family medical guides) but that the library has no resources covering another aspect of the same subject (e.g., childbirth guides)" (Vogel 1996, p. 72). Second, libraries must often pay for electronic resources and print resources out of the same budget. By incorporating electronic resources into a comprehensive policy for the institution, the librarian can view "funding for purchase of materials as an integrated unit out of which both print and electronic resources are purchased" (Vogel 1996, p. 67).

Those who advocate creating a separate policy for electronic resources feel that it should be used in conjunction with a traditional policy. A specific electronic collection development policy often focuses more on the format and cost of the specific resource as opposed to the traditional policy which looks at how well an item fits into or supports a collection. Penn State Harrisburg is one institution that has developed a separate *Collection Development Statement for Electronic Information Resources*, with a primary goal of setting parameters for choosing between print format, electronic format, or both (White and Crawford 1997).

Each library is unique and thus its policy statement will be unique.

Examples abound in the field as to how to incorporate electronic resources into a policy statement. In 1993-94, the ALA RUSA CODES Collection Policy Committee collected policy statements from eighteen academic, public and special libraries and subsequently prepared a checklist of the most common elements that libraries have included in their collection development policy statements for selecting electronic resources (Fedunok 1996). Institutions as diverse as McGill University (www.library.mcgill.ca/collect/collect.htm) and University of Oregon (http://darkwing.uoregon.edu/~chadwelf/police.htm) have made their policies available on the Web. There are countless journal articles detailing specific institution's experiences as well as the COLLDV-L listserv which addresses collection development issues.

Whether a library has one overall collection development policy statement for the institution or separate policies for traditional and electronic resources, the policy statement(s) cannot be static documents. A regular review of the policy statement should be incorporated into a planning cycle that, ideally, coincides with license renewals for significant electronic resources in the collection (Johnson 1996). The existence of a current, written policy is an advantage to librarians. It provides them with guidelines and justification for decisions made when they are challenged.

LIBRARIANS' EXPERIENCES

To this point the focus of this paper has been on the differences between print and electronic resources, selection criteria, and modifications to collection development policies. All have been discussed in the literature in detail. While there are many collection development policy statements for specific institutions available for perusal, there are fewer real life experiences documented in the literature that address the essential question: Are librarians canceling print subscriptions in favor of electronic resources? Those that have answered the question show that the replies vary widely as do the reasons for the answers.

In 1996, when asked, "How are you handling decisions about electronic resources versus print resources?" (Cassell, Interview with Joan Grant, 1996, p. 38), the Director of Collection Services at the Bobst Library at New York University responded that they duplicate print and electronic versions for standard indexing tools. Print is often canceled if the same material is available on CD-ROM, however "to date we have not canceled many print subscriptions" (Cassell, Interview with Joan Grant, 1996, p. 38).

A survey of academic librarians conducted in 1994 studied in detail the issue of dual subscriptions to print and CD-ROM formats of periodical indexes. Seventy percent of the responding academic libraries had canceled print subscriptions; the average number canceled was seven. The print index subscriptions were not canceled because an equivalent electronic resource became available but because of infrequent use of the print material. Cost was the second determining factor as to whether to retain the print version of a CD-ROM product. Many librarians were concerned about the fact that vendors charge more for CD-ROM products to non-subscribers of the print index than to subscribers (Condic and Lepkowski 1994).

Cost is a central issue for many librarians. A study conducted at the University of the Pacific Libraries focused on a cost/benefit analysis of owning a periodical versus having access to its contents through an online full-text periodical database. The researchers concluded that access to the full-text database allowed the library to offer more than twice as many journals than it had been with only a 15% increase in costs. The library's decision was to obtain a one-year trial subscription to the full-text database but at the same time continue all print subscriptions. After the one year period they intended to cancel most of the duplicated print materials if the experiment proved to be a success as measured by cost savings and the impacts on staff and users (Hawbaker and Wagner 1996).

At Columbia University Libraries the coordinator of collection development indicates that the library participates in consortium buying to reduce the costs of digital resources. The library has developed a five-year plan that outlines specific goals for the collection of electronic resources. "At the moment we have 5 percent of the collection in digital form and are spending about $500,000. We plan to have 11 percent of our collection in digital form by 2002 and be spending about $1,000,000. This will mean an annual cut of $80,000 in the periodicals budget" (Cassell, Interview with Anthony Ferguson, 1998, p. 41). However, it is mentioned that not all users want electronic resources, so the library will need to have both print and electronic available with some necessary duplication.

The libraries most likely to drop print materials in favor of electronic resources are special libraries. The reasons given for this include the fact that organizations often need to gather information quickly and are willing to pay for and can absorb the costs of an online search more easily than a public or academic library. Organizations also have limited space for storage of print materials. Access to online resources expand their access to information and thus are a more favorable option (Machovec 1990).

For those print resources that are also available in an electronic format, there are those who ask: Why do we *have* to choose? Most librarians believe that "there will always be a place for the book (Cassell, Interview with Merle Jacob, 1996, p. 26). In fact, current financial information for the SUNY Libraries illustrates the continued importance of print material. Based on a 1996 survey, the acquisitions budget was approximately $32,000,000–only $2,300,000 was spent on electronic resources (Schumacher 1998). At one campus, SUNY-Albany, the number of books bought continues to increase. In 1994-95 the number of English language approval plan books acquired was 6620. In 1997-98 that figure rose to 9030 (Miller 1998). Some carry their arguments to the extreme and insist that two libraries are needed today, one electronic and one book–one kind of library does not have to be "destroyed to create another" (Boardman 1996, p. 19). There should be a deliberate attempt to promote both kinds of media, "not just focus on what interests and excites us most at the moment . . . We need to let computers do what they do best and let print do what it does best" (Boardman 1996, p. 19). There are instances where the print product is considered a "core publication" and while "an electronic version may improve access, the presence of the printed product may be crucial for public relations" (Machovec 1990, p. 27).

CONCLUSION

In the midst of all the discussions supporting one type of resource over another or advocating the collection of both, there are those who assert that it is not relevant whether the desired information is available online or on CD-ROM or in print, it is the *content* that is important. "Libraries cannot avoid the hardware, software, and access issues, but if we place too much importance on them, we may miss the content" (Davis 1997, p. 395). "It is the information that determines the format not the reverse" (Aston 1996, p. 239).

There are readily identifiable differences between print and electronic resources. It is important to understand them and realize that each information format has strengths and weaknesses. There are many variables to consider and, because each situation is unique, what is crucial to one library is less important to another. Selection criteria can help define the variables and the use of a decision matrix can enable a selector to collect all needed information into a framework that allows for easier comparison and decision making. A collection development policy statement that incorporates electronic resources is a necessity. Not only does it provide guidance in the selection of materials but helps assure that the collection of those materials supports the mission and goals of the library. Equally important, a written policy can support the actions of a library if objections are raised about the content of the collection. The experiences shared by today's librarians illustrate the complexity of the selection dilemma. There is no consensus, no right way to make a decision about whether to retain print materials, discard them in favor of electronic products or include both in a collection. These will be addressed many times over as electronic product offerings continue to grow and gain acceptance and as cost, perhaps, becomes less of an issue. For now, however, "there is not a single simple answer" (Machovec 1990, p. 26).

REFERENCES

American Library Association (1987), *Guide for Writing a Bibliographer's Manual*, American Library Association, Chicago, IL.

Aston, Jennefer. "The Selection Dilemma." *Law Librarian* 27 (1996) : 238-41.

Boardman, Edna M. "We Need Two Libraries: One Electronic, One Book." *The Book Report* 14 (March/April 1996): 17-19.

Campbell, Stan. "A diminished thing: What are we losing by favoring electronic access?" *College & Research Libraries News* 59.4 (April 1998): 263-64.

Cassell, Kay Ann. "Interview with Anthony Ferguson, Columbia University Libraries." *Collection Building* 17.1 (1998): 40-41.

Cassell, Kay Ann. "Interview with Joan Grant, Director of Collection Services, Bobst Library, New York University." *Collection Building* 15.2 (1996): 36-38.

Cassell, Kay Ann. "Interview with Merle Jacob, adult materials selection specialist, Chicago Public Library." *Collection Building* 15.1 (1996): 24-26.

Caywood, Carolyn. "Selection Criteria for World Wide Web Resources." *Public Libraries* 35 (May/June 1996): 169.

Choice 36.2 (Oct. 1998).

"Collection Development Policies." n. pag. Online. Internet. 8 Nov. 1998. Available http://darkwing.uoregon.edu/~chadwelf/police.htm.

Compton, Lawrence E. "A Study of the Use of CD-ROM Computer Systems and

Print Indexes at the University of Georgia Main Library" (ERIC Document Reproduction Service, ED 333 892, 1991).

Condic, Kristine Salomon and Frank J. Lepkowski. "Attitudes of Academic Librarians Toward CD-ROM Indexes and Print Cancellation." *RQ* 34.1 (1994): 48-58.

Davis, Trisha L. "The Evolution of Selection Activities for Electronic Resources." *Library Trends* 45.3 (1997): 391-403.

Duranceau, Ellen. "Beyond Print." *The Serials Librarian* 1 (1998) : 83-106.

Fedunok, Suzanne. "Hammurabi and the Electronic Age: Documenting Electronic Collection Decisions." *RQ* 36.1 (1996): 86-90.

Gupta, Usha. "CD-ROM Database Selection and User Education." *Arkansas Libraries* 50.4 (1993): 5-7.

Hawbaker, A. Craig and Cynthia K. Wagner. "Periodical Ownership Versus Fulltext Online Access: A Cost-Benefit Analysis." *The Journal of Academic Librarianship* 22 (March 1996): 105-09.

Johnson, Peggy. "Selecting Electronic Resources: Developing a Local Decision-Making Matrix." *Cataloging & Classification Quarterly* 22.3/4 (1996): 9-24.

Kluegel, Kathleen. "Redesigning Our Future." *RQ* 36.3 (1997): 330-34.

LaGuardia, Cheryl and Stella Bentley. "Electronic Databases: Will Old Collection Development Policies Still Work?" *Online* 16 (1992): 60-63.

Machovec, George S. "The Retention of Print Sources In View of Electronic Databases." *Colorado Libraries* 16 (1990): 26-28.

Martin, Katherine F. and Robert F. Rose. "Managing the CD-ROM Collection Development Process: Issues and Alternatives." *Collection Management* 21.2 (1996): 77-102.

"McGill Libraries Collections Policies." n. pag. Online. Internet. 8 Nov. 1998. Available www.library.mcgill.ca/collect/collect.htm.

Miller, Heather. Guest Speaker for ISP 606. SUNY-Albany. 27 Oct. 1998.

Nisonger, Thomas E. "The collection development literature of 1996: A bibliographic essay." *Collection Building* 17.1 (1998): 29-39.

Pastine, Maureen. "Introduction." *Collection Management* 21.2 (1996): 1-30.

Ratzer, Mary. Head Librarian at Shenendehowa High School Library, Clifton Park, New York. Personal interview. 6 Nov. 1998.

Schumacher, John. Guest Speaker for ISP 606. SUNY-Albany. 10 Nov. 1998.

Vogel, Kristin D. "Integrating Electronic Resources into Collection Development Policies." *Collection Management* 21.2 (1996): 65-76.

White, Gary W. and Gregory A. Crawford. "Developing an electronic information resources collection development policy." *Collection Building* 16.2 (1997): 53-57.

Locating Moving Image Materials
for Multimedia Development:
A Reference Strategy

Rebecca S. Albitz

SUMMARY. With the growing interest in multimedia development and use, both by students and faculty members, the need to locate moving image materials to illustrate these projects will grow as well. This article outlines the resources, both print and electronic, and strategies the reference librarian can use to assist the client in locating the desired materials, in libraries, stock footage libraries, or archives. The implications of incorporating copyrighted material into a multimedia project designed for non-commercial, educational use are also discussed. *[Article copies available for a fee from The Haworth Document Delivery Service: 1-800-342-9678. E-mail address: <getinfo@haworthpressinc.com> Website: <http://www.HaworthPress.com>]*

KEYWORDS. Multimedia, multimedia development, moving images–reference, videorecordings, motion pictures–archives

INTRODUCTION

As evidence that visual resources have become essential to many areas of teaching and research, students may be asked to create a

Rebecca S. Albitz (BA, MA in Film Studies; MLS) is Head Librarian, The Pennsylvania State University Shenango campus.

Address correspondence to: Rebecca S. Albitz, 147 Shenango Avenue, Sharon, PA 16146 (E-mail: rsa4@psu.edu).

[Haworth co-indexing entry note]: "Locating Moving Image Materials for Multimedia Development: A Reference Strategy." Albitz, Rebecca S. Co-published simultaneously in *The Reference Librarian* (The Haworth Information Press, an imprint of The Haworth Press, Inc.) No. 71, 2000, pp. 99-110; and: *New Technologies and Reference Services* (ed: Bill Katz) The Haworth Information Press, an imprint of The Haworth Press, Inc., 2000, pp. 99-110. Single or multiple copies of this article are available for a fee from The Haworth Document Delivery Service [1-800-342-9678, 9:00 a.m. - 5:00 p.m. (EST). E-mail address: getinfo@haworthpressinc.com].

multimedia presentation as a final project so as to demonstrate both a knowledge of the subject matter and an ability to apply new technologies. Instructors in all disciplines now incorporate visual images into their curricula. Many have moved beyond showing videos or projecting slides to developing their own multimedia programs in order to engage their students visually, both on campus and via distance education technologies. Researchers also use visual images as objects of study, per se, even in fields outside of film or media studies. Thus, the challenge for the reference librarian becomes helping students, instructors, and researchers locate the appropriate visual materials, while keeping in mind that clients bring different needs and resources with their requests for assistance. Accordingly, this article discusses a number of different reference sources, both print and electronic, a librarian can consult to locate moving media titles to be purchased or rented or accessed from stock footage libraries or archives. The article also discusses the legal implications involved in incorporating copyrighted visual materials into multimedia projects designed for non-profit, educational use.

For the purposes of this discussion, the phrase "commercially available moving image materials" refers to films or videos that are currently available for purchase or rental, primarily feature films and documentaries. "Stock footage and archival film or video" refers to those moving image materials housed exclusively in a stock footage library or available only through an archive.

COMMERCIALLY AVAILABLE MOVING IMAGES–PRINT RESOURCES

Rich sources of moving images, commercially available films and videos can be incorporated easily into a multimedia presentation. A feature film may dramatize a moment in history to enhance a classroom presentation. Documentaries and educational films often contain images that illustrate certain scientific principles. Video is, in particular, easy to acquire, once one has identified an appropriate title, since video production companies like to publicize their products and make them available to consumers. In fact, because of the ease of acquisition and relatively inexpensive cost, one should think first of video as a resource for one's moving image clients. Nevertheless, since sections of films and videos are rarely indexed, the task for both the client and

the librarian becomes determining which feature or documentary contains the desired illustrative scenes. At best the reference sources
discussed here provide general, overarching subject headings for documentary titles, but little if any subject guidance to feature films.
Clients must often view a title to locate appropriate images.

Directories. Librarians know well the process used to locate a book
and determine if it is available for purchase. *Books in Print* (BIP),
which includes all titles currently in print and available for purchase,
is the standard source for locating United States imprints. Unfortunately, no single source exists when one sets out to search for video
recordings or films by title, and no single source lists commercially
produced moving media titles by subject, the avenue a student or
instructor would be most likely to follow. Two commonly used print
directories for in-print videos available for purchase are *Bowker's
Complete Video Directory* and *The Video Source Book* (1998; 1997/
1998). Used together, these two guides serve as a single *Books in Print*
for video recordings; alone, neither can claim to be as comprehensive
as *BIP*. While primarily sources for video publication information
(video producer, director and distributor), these directories provide
limited subject access for documentary or educational titles. Rather,
they use such broad subject headings such as "nursing," "reptiles and
amphibians," and "puppets." Each directory organizes its feature
films in a different way. *Bowker's* groups feature or entertainment
films by such genres as comedy or children's programming. *The Video
Source Book* does not include a separate genre section for feature
films; it groups features with the educational films under their broad
subject headings, and highlights the feature films, allowing a user to
distinguish them from the educational titles.

A similar source for both 16mm films and videos available from
university-operated rental collections exists. These collections contain
many titles no longer in distribution and, therefore, unavailable for
purchase. *The Film and Video Finder* lists title information gathered
by the National Information Center for Educational Media (NICEM)
(1997). These titles are available for rent through members of The
Consortium of College and University Media Centers (CCUMC). The
print version of *The Film and Video Finder*, like *The Video Sourcebook* and *Bowker's*, provides title access, but its subject access is more
thorough. It provides major subject groupings, with more specific
subheadings. For example, "reptiles" as a subject belongs under the

broader heading "biological sciences," rather than as a separate heading unto itself, as is the case with *Bowker's*. Also, relying on various interfaces including SilverPlatter and DIALOG, NICEM uses its holdings files to generate different electronic products. These CD-ROM and online versions of *The Film and Video Finder* help a researcher employ keyword searching and rely, as well, on the subject thesaurus developed by NICEM, incorporating both Sears and Library of Congress subject headings.

Video Guides. The video guide provides a more focused print resource for subject information about commercially produced media resources. A variety of publishers have compiled several subject guides, the most recent and prolific being Facets Multimedia. Facets, a Chicago-based video distribution company, stocks a wide variety of feature and documentary video titles. It organizes its main print catalog by geographic regions and general subject areas and has published segments of this catalog as individual books. Two of Facets' best-known titles include *Facets Gay and Lesbian Video Guide* and *Facets African American Video Guide* (McGavin 1994; Ogle 1997). By searching Library of Congress subject headings and using "video catalogs" as a subject modifier, one can locate these guides organized by specific subjects in a library through one's on-line public access catalog (OPAC). For example the subject heading for a video guide on dance would be "dance–video catalogs"; or a video guide focusing on teaching management would be "management–study and teaching–video catalogs." Because of the fluidity of the video market–videos tend to come into and go out of print quickly–these guides can become outdated within a couple of years. Also, while their titles allow a researcher to locate video titles grouped by broad subject headings, once again the specific actions or events a student or instructor might require remain unindexed.

COMMERCIALLY AVAILABLE MOVING IMAGES– ON-LINE RESOURCES

In those libraries with extensive video collections, the local OPAC should be the first resource a student or instructor explores. Most academic libraries include Library of Congress subject headings in their cataloging records for media materials, which helps the client identify potentially useful media resources.

In those libraries without access to a local media collection, on-line resources can expedite a search for videos and films acquired by other libraries. Both OCLC and RLIN list materials cataloged by member libraries, and depending upon the interface one uses to access either of these union catalogs, some keyword searching is available. OCLC WorldCat is the more comprehensive of these two union catalogs, containing more than 30 million records for items held at participating libraries around the world. More than 900,000 of these entries record visual materials. OCLC's catalog includes records for a broad variety of libraries–public, academic, and special–unlike RLIN, which focuses on the holdings of research libraries. When using either of these databases, one can search Library of Congress subject headings if they are included in a video's cataloging record.

Once a librarian locates an appropriate commercially produced video or film, three options present themselves. The first is to purchase the video for the student or faculty member. The second is to request the title through interlibrary loan, assuming the holding library is willing to lend its videos or films to other libraries. The third is to rent the title from a rental library, like those whose collections appear in *The Film and Video Finder*. These three options definitely increase the chances of obtaining a desired title. While locating a film or video that is still in general circulation can be a challenge, it is certainly easier than attempting to locate a title not housed in an academic or public library. The next section will outline reference sources that can be used to locate moving image materials available from stock footage libraries and film/video archives.

STOCK FOOTAGE LIBRARIES–
PRINT AND ONLINE RESOURCES

If the student or instructor is pressed for time, and is willing to pay for the use of the images they need, then stock footage libraries are excellent resources to explore. Because they are in the business of making their materials available for purchase, stock footage libraries provide excellent subject access to their collections. Many stock footage collections have print catalogs which can be acquired by contacting the company directly. Some have also created web sites that allow potential customers to search for the exact images they need. Most of these sites have keyword searching capabilities. When a record containing the sought-for word or phrase is retrieved, the record will usually give a shot-by-shot breakdown of the scenes contained within the described segment. Some of these sites even allow the potential customer to preview a portion of the footage via the Internet before making a decision to purchase. To locate stock footage World Wide Web sites, the best resource to use is Footage.net at http://www.footage. net. Footage.net has an extensive alphabetical list of stock footage libraries, and provides access to those companies that have web sites. Entries for those companies that do not have official web sites contain addresses and phone numbers, and some have e-mail addresses listed with Footage.net. The costs associated with using stock footage materials depend on a number of factors, including length of the clip, how the clip will be used, and licensing fees.

FILM AND VIDEO ARCHIVES

Perhaps the most difficult materials to locate are those housed in film and video archives. And, once located, archival film is rarely available for purchase or duplication. So, why would a student or researcher be interested in these materials? In most cases a student will not be interested, as accessing materials in film archives requires travel to the facility, and once there, the student will probably not be able to reproduce the images they locate. Researchers, on the other hand, usually have more financial resources available to them that allow for travel and, if permissible, duplication fees. If they are seeking a very specific image from a film, the researcher's only option may be an archive. Although the availability of both documentary and feature films on video expands continuously, those titles that do not have a broad audience, and thus do not guarantee a distributor cost recovery opportunities, are rarely released on video. Also, if the physical holder of a film does not have clear copyright ownership of the title, then they do not have the right to redistribute a title on video. Archives become the only source for these materials. Like commercially available films and videos, however, archival films are not indexed in any truly systematic manner, which is why a visit to the facility is necessary.

There are, of course, some archives that are in the business of providing moving images to the researcher and scholar at nominal fees based primarily on reproduction costs. These archives tend to focus on news or news related materials, such as the CSPAN archives housed at Purdue University (http://www.pava.purdue.edu), The Vanderbilt News Archives housed at Vanderbilt University (http://tvnews.vanderbilt.edu), and The Julian P. Kanter Political Commercial Archive housed at the University of Oklahoma (http://www.ou.edu/pccenter/archives/archival.html). Because they are working with materials that are usually not copyrighted, these archives are often able to sell copies of their holdings to researchers and scholars for relatively small fees. These collections are also well indexed, allowing the user easy access to moving image materials sought.

ARCHIVAL FILMS AND VIDEOS–PRINT RESOURCES

There are a number of print resources available to those who are seeking film or video titles housed in archives. Although some of these sources do not provide catalogs of exact title holdings, many outline categories of film types that the archive collects, including collection strengths and special holdings. The most complete and readily updated is the *Footage* series, published by the same company that operates Footage.net (1997). The first edition of this source was published in 1989, with a supplement appearing in 1991 and a new edition in 1997. *Footage* entries are organized by company or archive, with information about contacts, access, and licensing. A description of the overall collection is offered, focusing on strengths and offering general holdings information by subject categories. These categories are used as subject access points, organized as a subject index at the end of the publication.

While *Footage* has been updated twice since its initial publication, there are a number of other published archive surveys that have not been updated as frequently. Some examples of these directories or catalogs are: *The International Directory of Film and TV Documentation Collections*; *Motion Pictures, Television, and Radio: A Union Catalogue of Manuscript and Special Collections in the Western United States*; and *Scholar's Guide to Washington D.C. Media Collections* (Beauclair and Goldman 1994; Mehr 1977; Rowan and Wood 1994). While certainly useful to the serious media scholar who plans to visit archives in a specific region, these titles may not be as useful to those who plan to incorporate images into a class project or instructional tool.

ARCHIVAL FILMS AND VIDEOS–ONLINE RESOURCES

With the proliferation of the Internet, there are many reference sources one can use to locate archival film or video, even if the print resources mentioned in the previous section are not available. In fact these electronic sources are easier to use than their print counterparts, as they usually offer keyword searching capabilities.

There are at least two World Wide Web metasites that provide access to a list of film archive web sites. One is Footage.net at http://www.footage.net and the other is through the Library of Congress at http://lcweb.loc.gov/film/arch.html. Each of these locations offers links to those archives that have established web pages. While each archive's web site differs, many provide a keyword search mechanism. They also describe their access and duplication policies, if they allow duplication at all. Either of the web sites mentioned above would be an excellent place to begin a search for a film or video housed in an archive.

Of course there are many moving image titles housed in facilities other than film archives. If the researcher is seeking regional footage, then a call to the local historical society might prove beneficial. If historic footage featuring a company or organization is needed, contacting the archive for the group or institution should be more successful than searching a film-specific archive. Most archives and special collections have some moving image media, whether documentaries, home movies or industrial films, and are happy to make them available to researchers, depending on the condition of the item.

LISTSERVS

The resources outlined above are useful in determining what subject or area an archive may specialize in, or who may distribute a video recording for purchase. Rarely will archives advertise the availability of specific titles in their collection, which is particularly true if you are searching for a feature film. And, locating out-of-print video titles can seem impossible, because the commercial video market is so dynamic. When seeking a specific film title, the most efficient way to locate it is often via an Internet listserv or discussion group. A number of scholarly and professional groups exist for those interested in a film or video for research or teaching, including AMIA-L (the Association of Moving Image Archivists–AMIA-L@LSV.UKY.EDU), H-Film (History and Film–H-FILM@H-NET.MSU.EDU), and Screen-L (The Society for Cinema Studies–SCREEN-L@UA1VM.UA.EDU), and Video-lib (The Video Round Table, an American Library Association organization–VIDEOLIB@LIBRARY.BERKELEY.EDU). Members who subscribe to these lists are quite knowledgeable about conducting film research, and either run or have spent a great deal of time conducting research in moving image archives and video collections. For example, a query on one of these listservs requesting footage of the Dreamland Amusement Park in Coney Island received an immediate response suggesting a video about Coney Island that aired as part of the American Experience series on PBS.

COPYRIGHT ISSUES

All of the reference resources described above will aid the student, instructor, or researcher in locating the images needed to complete a multimedia project. If the materials are found in a stock footage library, then incorporating these images into another product is not an issue. Part of the fee stock footage libraries charge compensates the copyright holder for the use of their material. Film archives will each have a different policy in place addressing use issues, to which the client will have to adhere. Use of commercially available materials is a bit more complex, however, as issues of fair use for educational institutions come into play.

> Although current copyright law and practice permits a broad privilege to use and reproduce copyrighted works in non-profit educational institutions without seeking permission from the copyright holder and paying royalties, it does not generally exempt the teacher/developer of a multimedia work from obtaining permission from the copyright holder to incorporate portions of copyrighted works into multimedia programmes. (Gasaway 1997, 154)

Multimedia developers are currently working with two documents that guide their judgement when using copyrighted materials: the fair use concept in the Copyright Law and the proposed Fair Use Guidelines for Educational Multimedia.

Fair use was incorporated into the US copyright law during a 1976 revision. The fair use statement reads:

> [T]he fair use of a copyrighted work, including such use by reproduction in copies or phonorecords or any other means specified by that section for purposes such as criticism, comment, news reporting, teaching (including multiple copying for classroom use), scholarship or research, is not an infringement of copyright. In determining whether the use made of a work in any particular case is a fair use the factors to be considered shall include–
>
> 1. the purpose and character of the use, including whether such use is of a commercial nature or is for nonprofit;
> 2. the nature of the copyrighted work;
> 3. the amount and substantiality of the portion used in relation to the copyrighted work as a whole; and
> 4. the effect of the use upon the potential market for or value of the copyrighted work. The fact that a work is unpublished shall not itself bar a finding of fair use if such finding is made upon consideration of all the above factors (Besenjak 1997, 186).

The statement of fair use and these four criteria, along with the copyright law as a whole, have been the general measure by which fair use has been determined within educational institutions. In 1994 a dialog began among members of the Consortium of College and University Media Centers (CCUMC), copyright holders, educators, and librarians now called the Conference on Fair Use (CONFU). One of the goals of CONFU was to establish fair use guidelines for the use of copyrighted materials in not-for-profit educational multimedia productions which all could agree upon. These guidelines were completed in July of 1996; the text is available on-line at http://www.indiana.edu/~ccumc/mmfairuse.html. These guidelines have been endorsed by the Subcommittee on Courts and Intellectual Property, Committee on the Judiciary, US House of Representatives, although they are not the law and therefore are not legally binding. A number of library and educational organizations, however, do not support the restrictive limitations on the amount of copyrighted materials that can be incorporated into a multimedia production that these guidelines specify. A number of other organizations, including the Association of American Colleges and Universities and the Special Library Association, have endorsed and are encouraging the implementation of the CONFU fair use guidelines within their member organizations.

The confusion over the amount of a copyrighted work that can be incorporated into a multimedia package designed for non-profit educational use will continue until all parties involved–copyright holders, libraries, academic institutions, and legislators–agree on a specific definition of fair use. Until that time many academic institutions have established their own copyright guidelines to which students and faculty members should adhere.

CONCLUSION

As the interest in multimedia technologies grows, the use of this technology will continue to flourish in educational institutions among both students and instructors. Assisting in the location of materials to aid in the production of such materials will become a challenge many more librarians will experience in all types of academic institutions. Access to those resources that will aid in locating commercially available video and film, stock footage, and archival materials, will greatly assist those who provide reference assistance to the campus' clientele interested in exploring new technologies and their applications to education.

REFERENCES

Beauclair, Rene and Nancy Goldman, eds. 1994. *The International Directory of Film and TV Documentation Collections*. London: FIAF Documentation Commission.

Besenjak, Cheryl. 1997. *Copyright Plain & Simple*. Franklin Lakes, NJ: Career Press.

Bowker's Complete Video Directory. 1998. New York: R.R. Bowker.

The Film and Video Finder. 1997. Albuquerque: National Information Center for Educational Media.

Footage: The Worldwide Moving Image Sourcebook. 1997. New York: Second Line Search.

Gasaway, Laura N. 1997. Fair Use for Faculty-created Multimedia. *Information & Communications Technology Law* 6: 153-173.

McGavin, Patrick Z. 1994. *Facets Gay and Lesbian Video Guide*. Revised and expanded by Gabriel Gomez. Chicago: Facets Multimedia, Inc./Academy Chicago Publishers.

Mehr, Linda Harris. 1997. *Motion Pictures, Television, and Radio, a Union Catalogue of Manuscript and Special Collections in the Western United States*. Boston: G.K. Hall.

Ogle, Patrick. 1997. *Facets African American Video Guide*. Chicago: Facets Multimedia, Inc./Academy Chicago Publishers.

Rowan, Bonnie G. and Cynthia J. Wood. 1994. *Scholar's Guide to Washington D.C. Media Collections*. Baltimore: Johns Hopkins University Press.

The Video Source Book. 1997/1998. Detroit: Gale Research.

Religious Studies on the Internet

William J. Bostrom

SUMMARY. Religious Studies is the "objective" side of human involvement with religion. One might believe or not believe the teachings presented, though it is hoped that the presentation is honest and fair. It can be maintained, however, that there is *always* a "subjective" element present when it comes to the relationship of people to God, or the gods or Ultimate Reality, and there are plenty of Internet sites devoted to the "subjective" practice of religion as well. However, this paper investigates how five major religions are presented "objectively" on the Internet: Judaism, Christianity, Islam, Hinduism and Buddhism. The presenters are the Religious Studies Departments of various American universities and the "Meta-Sites" recommended by them. It is found that the various scriptures are not, yet, well-presented for scholarly purposes on the Internet, as they are on some CD-Roms. Other aspects of Religious Studies fare better (e.g., presentations of major teachings, historical leaders and divisions of the five religions mentioned above). The Internet sites of the Religious Studies Department at the University of Wyoming and that of Professor James J. O'Donnell at the University of Pennsylvania seemed especially promising study resources. *[Article copies available for a fee from The Haworth Document Delivery Service: 1-800-342-9678. E-mail address: <getinfo@haworthpressinc.com> Website: <http://www.HaworthPress.com>]*

KEYWORDS. Religious studies, Internet, religious studies department sites, World Wide Web–religious sites, major world religions

Address correspondence to: Rev. William J. Bostrom, P.O. Box 1624, Lakeville, CT 06039.

[Haworth co-indexing entry note]: "Religious Studies on the Internet." Bostrom, William J. Co-published simultaneously in *The Reference Librarian* (The Haworth Information Press, an imprint of The Haworth Press, Inc.) No. 71, 2000, pp. 111-130; and: *New Technologies and Reference Services* (ed: Bill Katz) The Haworth Information Press, an imprint of The Haworth Press, Inc., 2000, pp. 111-130. Single or multiple copies of this article are available for a fee from The Haworth Document Delivery Service [1-800-342-9678, 9:00 a.m. - 5:00 p.m. (EST). E-mail address: getinfo@haworthpressinc.com].

"Finding God in Cyberspace" is the name of a guide to religious studies resources on the Internet (http://gabriel.franuniv.edu/jp2/fgic/contents.htm). Someone at the University of Notre Dame Theology Department's web site called it "a very rich resource that is not as hokey as its title." It is an excellent resource, and I would say that the title is more "attention grabbing" than "hokey"; but I agree with the Notre Dame reviewer that it is unlikely that God has a URL.

Another interesting site is "Rich Geib's Humble Outpost in Cyberspace (http://wwwrjgeib.com/thoughts/gibbon/gibbon.html)." There I found a quote in his "Thoughts Worth Thinking" section from Sir Edward Gibbon (1737-1794), the author of *The Rise and Fall of the Roman Empire*. Gibbon said:

> The various modes of worship which prevailed in the Roman world, were all considered by the people as equally true; by the philosopher as equally false; and by the magistrate as equally useful.

We may now call magistrates "politicians," but some things don't change much!

Similarly, we can find "Blaise Pascal's Memorial" and his "Wager" on the Internet. I found them through "Yahoo" and "Netscape." But the religious experience which led to his memorial in November of 1654 was his alone; and the "Wager" (i.e., "If God does not exist one will lose nothing by believing in him; while if he does exist one will lose everything by not believing.") brought up two sites which described it and about 25 sites which vehemently argued against it; but it was introduced by Netscape with a flashing advertisement for gambling sites (so much for the artificial intelligence of computer networks in this case)!

The Web is great for conveying information, but what people do with that information, certainly in the case of politics and religion, is beyond electronics alone. There is a distinction between the objective "study of" religion and the subjective "practice of" religion. The two are not identical; neither are they mutually exclusive; and they are both on the Internet. This paper is concerned with the former.

LIMITATIONS AND CRITERIA USED

I restricted my endeavor to the objective "study of" religion. My first step was to go to the "religious studies" departments of U.S.

colleges and universities and see what their web sites had to offer. I did not use any foreign sites as "starting points." This was an arbitrary decision because I had to start with some definable limits. I chose university "religious studies" departments mainly on the basis of authority/quality control, as it were.

Secondly, I decided just to look at the five "major" world religions–Judaism, Christianity and Islam (western) and Hinduism and Buddhism (eastern). This limitation was largely a matter of time, though, to a lesser extent, these are the religions I have some familiarity with from my own college studies.

Next, I was looking for information on (1) sacred writings, (2) basic teachings, (3) history and divisions or branches and (4) major figures or leaders.

Finally, besides religious studies departments themselves I would look at the sites to which they directed me.

As far as the criteria used, I found those suggested at a Capital University (Columbus, OH) web site to be good (http://www.capital. edu/person/afields/WEBEVL2.HTM). Among them were: (1) Do the producers of the site have expertise relative to the subject? (2) Is obvious or subtle bias evident? (3) Does the site tell you how to contact its authors? (4) When was the information on the site produced and updated? Were most of its links still active? Also, a web page at the University of North Dakota (Grand Forks, ND) had good "Criteria of Scholarship" listed: Clarity, Objectivity, Purpose, Content, Accessibility, Presentation and Effect upon your thinking. This last seems to indicate there are still a few lovers of Kierkegaard left (http://www. und.edu/dept/philrel/WebSites.html)!

A young girl, upon seeing for the first time, a crucifix on a church building, asked her mother, "Mommy, what is that man doing up there?" Some people might answer that question with fervent faith, others "matter of factly," still others with scorn or bitterness. I would hope to answer such a question about each of these five religions RESPECTFULLY. I don't think all religions are the same though they are quite similar in certain teachings. I am a Christian. However, I believe every person, Christian or non-Christian, religious or not religious deserves some respect. I do not believe we are guaranteed to find God in cyberspace nor have an experience like Pascal's while seated in front of our monitors, but there is value in finding out what other people believe and considering their reasons for believing it; and I think the Internet can be very useful in this way.

RELIGIOUS STUDIES DEPARTMENTS

I applied the above criteria to the sites of individual religious studies departments and, through them, to "meta-sites" which may or not have been connected with a university. "The Voice of the Shuttle," for example, is from the U. of Cal. Santa Barbara (http://humanitas. ucsb.edu/shuttle/religion.html), while "Academic Info/Religion" (http:// www.academicinfo.net/religindex.html) is independent. After this, I went to the sites which they recommended for the individual religions.

The best religious studies department sites I found were these:

> The University of Wyoming in Laramie,WY (http://august.uwyo. edu/religionet/er/DEFAULT.HTM)–This site was created by Professor Paul Flesher in conjunction with a basic course in religion and its introductory materials were excellent. He limited the course to the five major world religions and, for each, had information and links under these categories:

1. Organization–how the society was structured
2. Time & Worship–Holy Days and Seasons
3. Texts & Tales–sacred writings
4. Religious Life–"priesthood," common people, etc.
5. Life Stages–youth, adult, preparing for death
6. Timeline– history of the religion
7. Glossary
8. Terminology–how adherents refer to themselves
9. Maps–for different eras
10. Further Links–Here, the Jewish and Christian links were good, the Hindu were adequate, and the Buddhist and Muslim were minimal

This site was in support of a course, which I think is the most promising way in which to use the Internet. One needs face to face conversation and discussion opportunities, with "live" human beings, but as a supplemental source of information and email communication the Internet is good.

Bowdoin College Library in Brunswick, ME (http://www.
bowdoin.edu/dept/library/subj/religion/index.html)–This had separate sites listed for all the religions except Islam. However, they
had ten good sites listed under "General Sources," and Islam
was covered by these (e.g., "The Voice of the Shuttle" is quite
good on Islam). Also, Bowdoin's "Full-Text Resources" section
was quite good for the coverage of sacred writings. Bowdoin is
an example, often repeated, of a school's library supporting the
school's academic departments. Bowdoin's library site also had a
section called "Library Course Guides" which brought up introductory materials, links and course outlines for ten of the religion
courses taught at the college.

Colby College in Waterville, ME (http://www.colby.edu/rel/
resources.html)–This time Islam was given a separate section
with twelve sites, but Hinduism and Buddhism together were
only given five under a heading of "Asian Religions." They
were, however, nicely covered by the selections under "General
Electronic Resources (e.g., "Finding God in Cyberspace" and
TELA, *The Electronically Linked Academy*–http://scholar.cc.emory.
edu). *TELA*, in turn, had many links to WWW sites, including a
gopher site called "Alex: a catalog of electronic texts on the
internet" from North Carolina State University (URL too long to
get on the page); and so, on and on it seemed to go like those
little Russian wooden dolls that nest inside each other.

Agnes Scott College in Decatur, GA (http://www.scottlan.edu/
academic/fac_adv/relstudy.htm)–Unfortunately this page was
last updated in April, 1996, but they are still open and good links.
I confess that I had never even heard of this school. A friend, a
former dean at a woman's college in New York state, upbraided
me and said, "Sure, that's a good school. Get with it!" Well, they
were linked to fifteen sites including "Voice of the Shuttle at
UCSB and Pitts Theology Library at Emory University in Atlan-
ta, GA as well as to The Boston University School of Theology
(http://web.bu.edu/STH/Library/contents.html). This increased Agnes
Scott College's resources enormously. Being "well-connected"
electronically as well as financially would, thus, seem to be of
interest to college Boards of Trustees not to mention Admissions

Departments as a "selling point" to prospective students and donors.

A final small school which used their Internet links to good advantage was:

> Emmanuel College of Boston, MA (http://www.emmanuel.edu/library/religion.html)–Its "Cardinal Cushing Library" had only 8 religion links, but they were all good choices. The Virtual Religion Index out of Rutgers University, NJ, the "Christian Classics Ethereal Library from Wheaton College in IL and the independent, "Academic Info–Religion" I mention below.

There was also a link here to an interesting site called "World Scripture (http://www.rain.org/~origin/ws.html)." This had an excellent section summarizing the world's religions and their scriptures, but to me it seemed like an attempt to construct a new Tower of Babel (it must be my inherited fundamentalist genes). The site was sponsored by an organization called "United Communities of Spirit."

In essence, they cited a topic . . . say, "God," "Life after Death," or "Sin and Evil" and then quote scriptural sayings from various religious traditions to demonstrate, I suppose, that, deep down, all religions teach the same thing.

A lot of work and good intentions have gone into this site, but I, "Scrooge-like" perhaps, do not buy it. Certainly there are many similarities between religions, especially when it comes to how people should live with each other–ideas of not stealing, not murdering and of loving one's neighbor are fairly universal.

But there are differences which cannot be evaded. Atheism, pantheism and theism *do* contend against each other; as do incarnation and re-incarnation. Does respecting other people mean we have to live with the tension between their beliefs and ours, or does it mean we have to persuade everyone there *are* really no tensions? I think the former. However, this site does contain much good introductory information.

Among some of the larger or more prestigious universities the best sites I found were these:

> Department of Religious Studies at the University of California, Santa Barbara (http://www.religion.ucsb.edu/index.html)–This is a "gateway to over 500 college or university religious studies

departments in the U. S., and over 150 such departments world-wide." This site was begun early in 1996 and last updated in April, 1998. It is a comprehensive guide to these departments as well as to scholarly email discussion sites, religious studies journals and academic societies and to other "meta-sites" which may or not be connected with universities (e.g., Mike Madin's site once ran as "Comparative Religion" out of the University of Washington, but it is now the independent "Academic Info/ Religion." This is one of the places to begin looking for authoritative sites, of which I have listed only a few. It is well organized and comprehensive.

"Religion Religions Religious Studies" (http://www.clas.ufl.edu/ users/gthursby/rel/)–This is from Professor G. Thursby at the University of Florida, Gainesville, FL. I found this site quicker to get into than the UCSB site, better annotated and with a smaller section of judiciously selected links to Religious Studies Departments and Theological Schools. It also had a good, brief history of "U.S. Departments of Religion" and good theoretical articles about "religious studies and the internet." This site might be easier to use than UCSB, but it does not have the comprehensive listings of UCSB.

St. John's University Libraries/Theology and Religious Studies, Jamaica, NY (http://www.stjohns.edu/library/staugustine/Theology/ default.html)–This is a ten page listing of unannotated sites. The first six pages are of Roman Catholic sites, followed by two pages of other Christian denominations and the Bible. Finally come other religions and other theological libraries. For most things Catholic this is a good place to begin. I found it easier to use than Notre Dame or Georgetown.

There is, by the way, a massive book called *Catholicism on the Web* by Thomas C. Fox. It is described, and can be ordered, at "The National Catholic Reporter Online" (http://www.natcath.com/catweb.htm). Information about the book and its author can also be found at Saint Mary's college at Notre Dame, IN. Actually, I found St. Mary's to have the best collection of *annotated* sites to religion of any of the Catholic schools (http://www.saintmarys.edu/~incandel/funweb.html). It was called "Fun Religious Studies Web Sites" and had links to all sorts of places in which I was interested. Some of these were not scholarly sites, but others were; dealing even with Protestants like Luther, Wesley, C. S. Lewis and Dietrich Bonhoeffer (e.g., "Fides Quarens Internetum" at http://apu.edu/~bstone/theology/theology.html).

> "Virtual Religion Index" at Rutgers University, New Brunswick, NJ (http://religion.rutgers.edu/links/vrilist.html)–This may well be the best, most thorough guide to Religious Studies on the Internet. With links to scriptures, to introductions to the various religions, to fairly current scholarly articles to the official head-quarter sites of various religions, denominations and sects . . . this Index has them all. It has sections on "Archaeology," "Historical Studies," "Comparative Religion," "Psychology of Religion" and more. It seems to have every angle of looking at the subject covered. It is updated fairly often and past the first screen table of contents most of the links were well annotated.

I will single out one other large site, even though it is from a smaller school. This is the previously mentioned:

> "Finding God in Cyberspace" at Franciscan University in Steubenville, OH (http://gabriel.franuniv.edu/jp2/fgic/contents.htm)– It is not as massive as some of the other sites but it is just as well organized. It includes links to:

1. Print resources to:

   a. other Theological libraries, Christian and Jewish
   b. religious publishers and booksellers
   c. print journals of religion

2. People resources

   a. at scholarly societies
   b. at religious communities world-wide
   c. at scholarly online discussion groups

3. Various collections of electronic texts
4. Internet teaching resources
5. Gateways to Subject resources
   (e.g., Psychology of Religion or Religion and Literature)

6. Gateways to sites of the various religions themselves
   (e.g., Judaism and Jewish Resources)

As I said earlier, one won't find God's URL here, but it is a good place to learn about different belief systems.

If one is interested in *any particular* school's offerings in religious studies one should look up that school at the above mentioned UCSB site. There were many good sites listed there, but I will briefly mention five more that caught my attention.

First, "Religion Resources on the Web" at the University of California at San Diego (http:acusd.edu/theo/ref-gen.html)–This had good links, and also a good "Note to Students" cautioning students about biased sources on the web.

Second, The University of Pennsylvania, in Philadelphia, PA (http://ccat.sas.upenn.edu/rs/)–This had great links to religious art, good links to religious texts and a good section on the Branch Davidians of David Koresh.

Third, Vanderbilt University, Nashville TN (http://www.vanderbilt.edu/AnS/religious_studies/links.htm)–I think this may have had the best, brief listing of sites; only 2 pages.

Fourth, Michigan State University/Religious Studies Links, East Lansing, MI (http://pilot.msu.edu/user/religstu/reslinks.htm)–A wide variety of links to other beliefs as well as to the five major world religions; for example, to Asatru, Druidism, Goddess Worship and "The Urantia Book" among others.

Finally, Rhodes College Library at Memphis, TN (http://blair.library.rhodes.edu/relhtmls/relnet.html)–This had a very long list of sites for a small school; but they were well balanced for both major and minor world religions.

Large "Meta-sites" on religious studies were these:

"Voice of the Shuttle Web Pages for Humanities Research/ Religious Studies" (http://humanitas.ucsb.edu/shuttle/religion. html)–This is also from UCSB. Its selection of General Resources for Religious Studies and those for separate religious traditions are quite good, as well as its links to Religious Studies courses on the Internet (e.g., Diana Eck of Harvard University on "Hindu Myth, Image and Pilgrimage)."

"Academic Info on Religion"–Independent (http://www.academic info.net/religindex.html)–This has two indexes. An "Expanded Index" of 17 pages and a "Main Index" of three pages which gives way to over thirty pages of nicely annotated sites on the five major religions. It described the "Virtual Religion Index" from Rutgers U. as "the best site for the academic study of religion on the Internet. That is, indeed, true, but I preferred this one, as being clearer in its pages and more direct in getting to its links.

"World Lecture Hall: Religious Studies" from the University of Texas at Austin, TX (http://www.utexas.edu/world/lecture/rel/)– This had links to academic courses which are taught over the Internet from various schools. Especially good were "Augustine" from James J. O'Donnell at the University of Pennsylvania, "Buddhist Traditions" from James S. Dalton, Siena College, Loudenville, NY, and "Religions of the World–Eastern" from Charles Ess at Drury College, Springfield–MO.

There were many good foreign Meta-sites for the academic study of religion. For the most part, time-wise, they appear on screen as quickly as do the domestic sites, but I had to limit this study in some way so I didn't explore them thoroughly. Two academic Canadian sites, however, were frequently mentioned by the U.S. sites.

First was "General Religious Studies Resources on the Internet" from Edmonton, Alberta (http://fn2.freenet.edmonton.ab.ca/ca81/~cstier/religion/toc.htm)–Its opening page was brief, but nicely organized into "General Resources," "Western," "Eastern" and "Alternative Religions."

Secondly was the "APS Guide to Resources in Theology" from St. Michael's College, Toronto, Ontario (http://www.utoronto.ca/stmikes/theobook.htm)–Almost all the links were to Christian sites yet they had two good links to world religions in their "Textual Resources" section.

SEPARATE RELIGIOUS TRADITIONS

These I found to be the best sites as introductions to the five major world religions (history, teachings, people and scriptures):

Judaism

Introductions

"The Academic Jewish Studies Internet Directory" (http://www.
uni-duisburg.de/FB1/JStudien/jucont.htm)–Actually, this is a Ger-
man site which came up through AcademicInfo/Religion, but,
except for the arbitrary purpose of limiting the starting points of
this paper, there do not seem to be any boundaries to the World
Wide Web. This had great links to Academic Associations, Libraries, Research Institutes, Archives, Jewish Studies Programs
at Universities and "Other Useful Resources." It is the best
"gateway" to Jewish colleges and universities and seminaries
which I found.

"The Shamash Project/Judaism and Jewish Resources" (http://
shamash.org/trb/judaism.html)–This is a most comprehensive
guide to things Jewish, both academic and non-academic. Its
sections on "Jewish learning" [with links to the Tanach, Talmud
(both in Hebrew) and Torah with commentary (in English and
Hebrew)], to "Jewish studies" (a really excellent link to a course
from the U. of Cal./Davis on an "Introduction to Judaism") and a
section on "Hebrew" (e.g., how to configure Hebrew alphabet
characters to one's browser–if one is able to read Hebrew).

"Introduction to Judaism" (http://philo.ucdavis.edu/~bruce/RST23
homepage.html)–The course mentioned above. It includes sections on the subdivisions within Judaism and on Maimonides and
his "Basics of Judaism."

"Judaism 101" (http://members.aol.com/jewfaq/index.htm)–This
is a not so scholarly, but nevertheless, fairly comprehensive
introduction to Judaism.

Texts

"Scrolls from the Dead Sea" (http://sunsite.unc.edu/expo/deadsea.
scrolls.exhibit/intro.html)–A good introduction from some of the
oldest preserved documents in the world, and excerpts in English
from them too.

"Judaism of the Talmud and Midrash Index" (http://www.acs. ucalgary.ca/~esegal/RelS367/367_Index.html)–Apparently there is nothing yet in English except portions of the Talmud and Midrash. However, this site gives a good introduction to them.

"Documents of Jewish Belief" (http://www.netaxs.com/~expweb/ jewish_belief.html)–Good collection of historical texts from Maimonides "Thirteen Principles of Faith" to Rabbi Sholom Dov Ber Schneersohn's "Resurrection of the Dead."

I had difficulty finding sites with full expositions of Jewish sacred texts, either because they are so numerous or lengthy that no one has completed them yet, or else, because they are not in English, but in Hebrew. But the above sites give a fair introduction.

Christianity

Introductions

"Fides Quarens Internetum/Christian Theology Pages by Tradition" (http://apu.edu/bstone/theologytrad.html)–I checked out Catholic, Orthodox, Episcopal and Reformed links on this page and they all seemed to lead to good basic introductions to each of those traditions. There were about 35 traditions or denominations listed!

"The Christian Coptic Orthodox Church of Egypt" (http://cs-www. bu.edu/faculty/best/pub/cn/Home.html)–One of the smallest traditions within Christianity, this is also one of the oldest and they have long memories! This site is a listing of links seven pages long; and they haven't forgotten the rest of the church even if, as it often seems, they themselves are forgotten. A decent site to learn about Christianity's beginnings.

"Augustine" (http://ccat.upenn.edu/jod/augustine.html)–This is Professor James J. O'Donnell's web course from the University of Pennsylvania. I've always been fond of St. Augustine ever since I read his remark, "I doubt, therefore I exist; for he who does not exist cannot doubt." This is long before Descartes's more famous, "I think, therefore I am," or the Moody Blues version of

"I think, therefore I am . . . I think?" This is a very good course about a Christian thinker of great influence down through the centuries.

Texts

"Bible Gateway" (http://bible.gospelcom.net/bible?)–This allows one to look up passages of indeterminate length per book of the Bible (I was able to get all 66 chapters of Isaiah in), in seven versions in ten languages or look to up topics that a concordance will find. It is produced by Gospel Com.

"Biblical Studies Foundation–The Net Bible" (http://www.bible. org/)–Just in case some people get upset with the seven versions above here is a brand new one to infuriate them. A completely new version. Only in English. This site also has Calvin's *Institutes* on line!

"The Summa Theological of St. Thomas Aquinas" (http://www. knight.org/advent/summa/summa.htm)–Aquinas is also a thinker of long-lasting influence, and *The Summa* is his lasting bequest. Not everyone is still interested in "angels," except 1997/98 T.V. producers (and, perhaps, Mortimer Adler), but Thomas treats of them here in questions 50-64.

Christian Classics Ethereal Library (http://ccel.wheaton.edu/)–This is a truly impressive site. Not only does it have "The World Wide Study Bible" of nine versions with many commentaries, but also the 38 volume "Early Church Fathers." That's a $500.00 set of books that I wouldn't have room for even if I did buy them! Then, they also have the major works of Aquinas, Augustine, Bunyan, Calvin, Dante and many, many others down to Wesley and Whitefield; plus Fiction by G. K. Chesterton, Dostoevsky, George MacDonald and Tolstoy *(Anna Karenina* and ten other shorter works)!

Islam

Introductions

In general, I found the sites for Islam quite good at having both introductory materials and textual materials (e.g., The Qur'an) combined into one site. Among the best Introductions I found were these:

"Islamic Studies, Arabic, and Religion Web Page of Professor Alan Godlas of the University of Georgia" (http://www.arches. uga.edu/~godlas/)–The best, most comprehensive site I found on Islam.

"Al-Muslim" (http://www.al-muslim.org/)–This site was recommended by Webster University of St. Louis, MO (http://www. websteruniv.edu/depts/religion/islam.html) as well as several other schools. Webster had seven good links to Islamic topics. "Al-Muslim" linked to a good introduction at the University of Kansas (http://www.eecs.ukans.edu/~nghoseh/islam.html) which included sections on the "Concept of GOD in Islam," "Jesus and Islam" and "Human Rights in an Islamic State," among others.

"About Al-Islam and Muslims" (http://www.unn.ac.uk/societies/ islamic/about/)–This had forty-two sections on such things as "Converts," "War," "What is Islam," "Palestine," and "Salman Rushdie" and "The Pillars of Islam."

"The Islam Page" (http://www.islamworld.net/)–This site is immense, and, as with most every Muslim site I found, it is clear these pages are written by confirmed believers. They are very forthright and open about their beliefs. "If you are not a Muslim, you should be!" That is the attitude expressed. I am not a Muslim, but the attitude is refreshing in an age of "Orwellian Newspeak." It does not at all detract from value of the information expressed. One can learn much about Islam here. The Qur'an is here as well as tools for searching in it; also, part of "The Sunnah (sayings and deeds of Prophet Muhammad)" and "The Hadith (reports of his sayings and deeds)."

Texts

"Islamic Texts and Resources MetaPage" (http://wings.buffalo. edu/student-life/sa/muslim/isl/isl.html)–This is divided into sections on "Introductions to Islam," "Scriptures and Prophetic Traditions" and "Islamic Thought" among others. It has links to translations of the Qur'an in English and other languages as well as to other historical writings. Actually, here I found the text of the Hindu Bhagavad-Gita, translated by Sir Edwin Arnold, as well as the Bible and Book of Mormon.

"The Koran" (http://www.hti.umich.edu/relig/koran/browse.html)–
This was the clearest English rendition of all 114 suras of the
Qur'an which I found.

"Translations of the Qur'an" (http://www.usc.edu/dept/MSA/
quran/)–Three translations of every verse are given–by Yusufali,
Pickthal and Shakir.

Hinduism

Introductions

"Hinduism"   (http://www.geocities.com/RodeoDrive/1415/indexd.
html)–This site was recommended by the Religion Studies Department at Lehigh University, Bethlehem, PA (http://www. lehigh.
edu/~inrel/inrel.html). It is a good, six page introduction to Hinduism with ample links coming off of it to explain terms like
"Veda," "Upanishads," "Advaita philosophies," etc.

"Advaita Vedanta Home Page" (http://www.cco.caltech.edu~vidya/
advaita/)–"The philosophy of advaita, literally non-dualism, is
the premier and oldest extant among Vedanta schools of Indian
philosophy."

"Hindu Tantric Page" (http://www.hubcom.com/tantric/)–This site
had great introductory material and many links to related WWW
sites. Suggested by Bowdoin College Library/Internet Resources/
Religion.

"Exploring Ancient World Cultures–India" (http://eawc.evansville.
edu/www/inpage.htm)–I cannot remember how I found this site,
but it has nine good links to India including Hindu religion. Also,
the University of Evansville, Evansville, IN, Department of Philosophy and Religion has excellent "WWW links to Religion
(http://cedar.evansville.edu/~philweb/showcase/)." I missed them
the first time around because of the (to me) unfamiliar term "show-
case." But, they are among the best selection of links I've found
so far.

"Hinduism" (http://wwwstud.uni-giessen.de/~s1925/hinduism. htm)–
This has a great "Main Index" to Hinduism which is quite comprehensive in covering teachings, texts and history."

Texts

"Bhagavad-Gita AS It Is" (http://www.krsna.com/gita/toc. html)–
This is an English Translation of the Hindu Classic by the "Found-
er-Acarya of the International Society for Krishna Consciousness."
This has a verse by verse transliteration, translation and commentary
on the Gita.

"The Song Celestial or Bhagavad-Gita" (gopher://gopher.vt.edu:
10010/02/96/1)–This is a very straightforward translation in English by Sir Edwin Arnold, which I mentioned above as getting
from the "Islamic Texts and Resource Page." This text is the
easiest one to read on the web unless you know Sanskrit!

"The Hindu Universe" (http://www.hindunet.org/scriptures)– This
site had many of the Hindu Upanishads, the Bhagwad Gita and
other texts in English. However, the Ramayana and Mahabharat
were in Sanskrit. This site was recommended by several universities and was a good place to go for an overall introduction to
Hinduism.

In general, I had difficulty finding many major Hindu texts in
English except for the Bhagavad-Gita and some of the Upanishads.

Buddhism

Introductions

"Virtual Religion Index" (Rutgers) (http://religion.rutgers.edu/links/
buddha.html)–They have good links to sites on "General Resources," "Siddhartha Gautama-the Buddha.," "Theravada,"
Mahayana," "Nichiren," "Shin," "Tibetan" and "Zen." This
seems to be a good place to begin searching, if you know more
than I do. For myself, the University of Wyoming site mentioned
above would be an introduction to help me use this introduction.

"Traditions and Schools of Buddhism" (http://www.interlog.
com/~klima/b/schools.html)–This had a very nice family tree
showing four stages in the development of Buddhism and which
division came from which. Many of these divisions were hyper-

text links to give you specific information on that particular sect of Buddhism.

"What is Theravada Buddhism?" (http://world.std.com/~metta/ theravada.html)–A good introduction to "The Lesser Vehicle" or "Southern Buddhism," the oldest form of Buddhism.

"Fundamental Buddhism Explained" (http://www.fundamental buddhism.com/)–This is a good introduction to the teaching of the Buddha and the subsequent history of Buddhism.

"Foundation for the Preservation of the Mahayana Tradition" (http:www.fpmt.org/Teachings/index.html)–This is a site where the thoughts of the Dalai Lama and other Lamas can be found. Mahayana is the "Greater Vehicle" or the "Northern Buddhism" of China, Japan, etc.

"A Short Guide to Tibetan Buddhism" (http://www.churchward. com/rel.html)–Vajrayana Buddhism is the "Diamond Vehicle" of the Himalayan regions. This site gives a brief history and links to other sites: one of the best summary introductions I found to the three major schools of buddhism was at "tibetan Buddhism (http://zip.com.au/~cee_gee/tibet.html)."

"Buddhist Basics: The ABC's of Buddhism" (http://www.tricycle. com/bddhismabcs.html)–This, too, was a very good, brief introduction to the history of Buddhism of three pages with a glossary of Buddhist terms of four pages.

Texts

"Yahoo/Society and Culture/Religion/Faiths and Practices/Buddhism/Teachings and Sutras (the URL is too long)–Several school departments of religion suggested the "Yahoo/Buddhism" index as being fairly thorough. It leads to many Buddhist texts.

"Dhammapada" (http://www.angelfire.com/ca/SHALOM/dham mapada.html)–The complete text of this basic scripture, but red letters on a black background are difficult to read!

"The Heart Sutra in English" (http://cres.anu.edu.au/~mccomas/ heartsutra/english.html)–An important scripture in Zen Buddhism.

"The Smaller Pure Land Sutra" (http://prairie.lakes.com/~lotusb5/ w3-trans/lesser-sukhavati.html)–Pure Land is the largest of any Buddhist sect in Japan.

"The Fire Sermon" (http://world.std.com/~metta/canon/samyutta/ sn35-28.html)–The Buddha's address to his disciples about the need to become disenchanted with the senses in their quest for nirvana.

"Primary Zen Texts" (http://www.io.com/~snewton/zen/primary-texts.html)–"Four Great Vows," "The Diamond Cutter Sutra," "The Four Noble Truths" and a few other Zen texts.

CONCLUSION

The University of Notre Dame had some good articles on "using the Internet for instructional purposes." These were listed as an introduction to their "On-Line Classes in the Department of Theology" section (http://www.nd.edu/~ktrembat/www-class/). Among them were:

"Rendezvous with the World–A Conversation with Dr. Kern Trembath" (http://www.nd.edu/~resnet/altern.html)–Dr. Trembath teaches "Foundations of Theology," a required course for Notre Dame undergraduates. He sees the Internet as reducing the distance between student and teacher, helping students to come to classes better prepared and improving classroom discussion.

"Instructional Uses and Effects of World Wide Web Course Pages: A Review of Instructor Experiences"–by Joseph M. Kayany (http://www.nd.edu:80/~ktrembat?AAHE/kayany.html)–Mr. Kayany is with the Department of Communication at Western Michigan University in Kalamazoo, MI. He reports the results of a survey among 78 college/university faculty who had used "web pages" as instructional tools. He found a shift in professors viewing themselves as a "sage on the stage" to becoming a "guide on the side." There are different types of web pages available (from a mere "syllabus with email information" to "Internet links with course resources"). "Computer expertise to design such a web page is becoming minimal," he says and there is password protection to protect the good student from becoming the victim of plagiarism by others.

"As Educators Rush to Embrace Technology, a Coterie of Skeptics Seeks to be Heard"–by Colleen Cordes (http://chronicle.com/colloquy/98/skeptics/background.htm)–Ms. Cordes appears to work for *The Chronicle of Higher Education.* Computers are strong for one kind of thinking–based on calculation and logic, but they do "nothing to enhance moral intuition, imagination, emotional thinking or a disciplined will. And there were many more "curmudgeonly" opinions expressed, many of which were worth considering.

Finally, I found a very positive proponent of the academic use of computers in Professor James J. O'Donnell of the University of Pennsylvania:

"New Tools for Teaching" (http://ccat.sas.upenn.edu/job/teach demo.html)–This is a long, multi-paged site that is extremely interesting and well-written. "Does one have to be an expert to write a web page?" "Will the students badger you to death with 'chit-chat on the email?'" Professor O'Donnell seems a brilliant, very productive fellow and I wonder, "Is he seeing the normal student accurately? Or is this Clark Kent forgetting that Jimmy Olsen is just Jimmy Olsen?" Then again, the U. Penn. graduates I've met are a whole lot more like Clark than Jimmy! Anyway, this is a great site with (realistic) high hopes for "Internet use in the classroom."

I think there is more value in the "introductory" aspects to instruction in religious studies than there is in presenting scriptures. From the standpoint of ergonomics my eyes wear out and my neck gets stiff if I have to look at a computer screen too long. The Internet is much better for shorter articles and email and pictures/images than it is for long texts. Then, too, technically, there does not yet exist on the Internet any products for searching in scriptures that are as good as some CD-Rom products. For example, I could find nothing like the product

"CDWord" for Bible research on the Internet; nor for any of the scriptures of the major religions. In fact, unless one knows Hebrew, Arabic, Sanskrit or Chinese those scriptures are closed for serious research.

However, Introductory materials are another matter. There are some very good print resources in this area right now, but the Internet, with its hypertext links and images can also be of value right now. The course at U. of Wyoming and the courses at U. of Pennsylvania are demonstrations of this. They won't replace print, but they can supplement it.

Finally, there will always be another "dimension" to religious studies. Personally, I have been instructed more about God and the human condition by thinking over *The Brothers Karamazov*, or *Brideshead Revisited* or *MacBeth* or *East of Eden* or, even, *The Spy Who Came in From the Cold*, than I ever have been by any "introductory" course in religion or any catechism class. For some people, it might be literature; for some, music; for others, simply being with people. There is a place for instruction. There is certainly a place for scriptures. But God has other ways too, even if that doesn't include a URL.

Kierkegaard and Pascal would understand.

SERVICE FOR WHOM?

Information Haves and Have Nots:
Small Thoughts on Large Themes

Joe Morehead

SUMMARY. The divide between information have and have-nots is highlighted by National Telecommunications and Information Administration studies. While more Americans have access to the Internet than ever before, a great majority of Blacks, Hispanics and other minorities lack such access. The role of libraries is this "information apartheid" situation is to provide free access to the Net and other technologies. A related matter: the question of domain names.

KEYWORDS. Internet access, information haves and have-nots, net domain names

Joe Morehead is the country's leading authority on government documents and is Professor, School of Information Science and Policy, SUNY/Albany, 135 Western Avenue, Albany, NY 12222. He is a frequent contributor to *The Reference Librarian.*

[Haworth co-indexing entry note]: "Information Haves and Have Nots: Small Thoughts on Large Themes." Morehead, Joe. Co-published simultaneously in *The Reference Librarian* (The Haworth Information Press, an imprint of The Haworth Press, Inc.) No. 71, 2000, pp. 131-143; and: *New Technologies and Reference Services* (ed: Bill Katz) The Haworth Information Press, an imprint of The Haworth Press, Inc., 2000, pp. 131-143. Single or multiple copies of this article are available for a fee from The Haworth Document Delivery Service [1-800-342-9678, 9:00 a.m. - 5:00 p.m. (EST). E-mail address: getinfo@haworthpressinc. com].

THE DIGITAL DIVIDE

The power and versatility of digital technology will raise . . . equity issues that will have to be addressed. The information society should serve all of its citizens, not only the technically sophisticated and economically privileged.

–Bill Gates, *The Road Ahead*

Is technology creating an even sharper divide between what is called the information haves and have nots? A series of studies by the National Telecommunications and Information Administration (NTIA), with the cooperation of the Census Bureau (both of which are agencies within the Department of Commerce), address the timeworn problem of an elitist few commanding the information industry (the geeks shall inherit the earth?) while a large majority of the great unwashed public lack the means to share in the plethora of wealth generated by computer technologies. Is this a new paradigm or simply a riff on the old information rich, information poor melody? Is this pouring old wine into new bottles (or vice-versa)? Is this, as Yogi Berra, undisputed master of the apposite tautology, might have said, deja vu all over again?[1]

According to its mission statement, the NTIA is the executive branch's principal voice on domestic and international telecommunications technology issues. The agency attempts to spur innovation, encourage competition, help create jobs, and provide consumers with more choices and better quality telecommunications products and services at lower prices. In less lofty terms, this means working to ensure that all Americans have affordable phone and cable service, especially the millions of people that reside in rural and underserved urban areas by means of information infrastructure grants. NTIA also provides the hardware that enables public radio and television broadcasters to maintain and extend the reach of their programming. Of course, public radio and TV is our oasis in a vaster expanse of the "vast wasteland" that Newton N. Minow famously deplored when he was chairman of the Federal Communications Commission during the presidency of John F. Kennedy. Other functions the agency is responsible for include advocating competition and liberalization of worldwide telecommunications policies and participating in government-to-government negotiations to open markets for United States companies. A full account of NTIA's mission along with an organization chart and staff directory is available on the agency's home page (http://www.ntia.doc.gov).

Falling Through the Net

Three NTIA reports have been published on the entity's Web site in the *Fin de siecle* decade of the twentieth century: July 1995, July 1998, and July 1999. In the 1995 report, titled *Falling Through the Net: A Survey of the "Have Nots" in Rural and Urban America*, NTIA surveyed trends in telephone subscribership, as well as ownership and usage of personal computers and modems using data obtained by the Census Bureau in its November 1994 *Current Population Survey*, a random sample of some 48,000 households. These data constituted the first census survey of its kind on PC/modem ownership. The second survey, titled *Falling Through the Net II: New Data on the Digital Divide*, updated the results of the 1995 report, again relying upon data compiled by the Census Bureau in October 1997. The third report in this series, named *Falling Through the Net: Defining the Digital Divide*, once again used Census Bureau data collected in December 1998 to provide an updated snapshot of the digital divide. Like the earlier two, the report examines which American households have access to telephones, computers, and the Internet, and which do not.

According to Larry Irving, NTIA's Assistant Secretary for Communications and Information, in an Introduction to the 1999 report, the digital divide "is now one of America's leading economic and civil rights issues."[2] What follows is a summary of the findings.

Good News/Bad News

The report states two ostensibly contradictory theses: more Americans have access to computers and the Internet than ever before in all demographic groups and geographic locations; yet the digital divide is still "significant," and in many instances has *widened* since the figures from the previous report were tabulated. First, the positive news. At the end of 1998, over 40 percent of American households owned computers, and one-quarter of all households had Internet access. Additionally, those who were less likely to have telephones (chiefly, young and minority households in rural areas) are now more likely to have phones at home. Nevertheless, the 1998 data reveal significant disparities, including the following:

- Households with incomes of $75,000 and higher are more than twenty times more likely to have access to the Internet than those at the lowest income levels, and more than nine times as likely to have a PC at home.
- Whites are more likely to have access to the Internet from home than African-Americans or Hispanics have from *any* location.
- African-American and Hispanic households are approximately one-third as likely to have home Internet access as households of Asian/Pacific Islander descent, and roughly two-fifths as likely as White households.
- Regardless of income level, Americans living in rural areas are lagging behind in Internet access. Indeed, at the lowest income levels, those in urban areas are more than twice as likely to have Internet access than those earning the same income in rural areas. The "least connected" groups are the rural poor, rural and central city minorities, households whose members are below age 25, and households headed by single-parent females.[3]

For many groups, the digital divide has widened as the information "haves" outpace the "have nots" in gaining access to electronic resources. The following gaps concerning home Internet access are representative:

- The disparities between White and Hispanic households, and between White and African-American households, are now more than six percentage points larger than they were in 1994.
- Between 1997 and 1998, the divide between those at the highest and lowest education levels increased 25 percent, and the variance between those at the highest and lowest income levels grew 29 percent.[4]

Apropos of income asymmetries, in September 1999, a think tank named the Center on Budget and Policy Priorities (http://www.cbpp. org) released a dispiriting study called *The Widening Income Gap*. The message: the rich are getting richer; the poor, poorer. "The poorest fifth of Americans have actually seen their after-tax income decline over the last 20 years. . . . The richest 2.7 million Americans now have as much income as the poorest 100 million."[5] That's a staggering statistic!

Information Apartheid

These trends, of course, are driven by technology, and if not halted and turned around might create an "information apartheid" that could instigate a "return to the class warfare of a century ago."[6] But the very companies that have developed these spectacular engines that drive the economy recognize "that the future market for their products depends upon the computer literacy of tomorrow's consumers." Cathy O'Rourke Smith, president of a technology communications firm based in Boston, says that "enlightened self-interest can be a tremendous force for good. If you look at Apple," she says, "that's a company that very early in its history realized that by putting its products in the classroom, it could create a whole generation of kids who grew up using the Mac operating system, comfortable with that system, but it also helped put computers in a lot of schools for the first time, and made a real contribution."[7]

In a 1997 discussion group posted to the Internet, optimistic comments on the status of the digital imbalance were voiced. The widening of the gap is, in the sanguine opinion of the moderators of this group, a temporary phenomenon. There is "an initial widening because it may take a while before computers are affordable enough for all schools to incorporate them into their academic programs. However, in keeping with Gordon Moore's Law (the price of a semiconductor chip halves every 18 months), we feel that eventually computers will become as commonplace and as inexpensive as television sets are today. Once this universal acceptance of computers takes place, we feel that the Internet will actually become the Great Equalizer. . . . We believe that [the computer] will enable even the poorest schools to remain competitive with the most wealthy schools." The panel makes an analogy to the business community:

> While during the pre-Internet times it was nearly impossible for small businesses to compete with large business, today such is not the case. This is because the Internet now makes it much, much cheaper for small businesses to compete. Advertising expenses are reduced and software applications that were once only affordable to large corporations are now available in client-server format for small businesses over the Internet. Just as small businesses are now able to compete with large corporations, so too will poor schools be able to compete with wealthy schools.[8]

Role of Libraries

In this setting libraries can play an important role. According to the 1998 data provided by the Census Bureau for the third *Falling Through the Net* report, Community Access Centers (CACs), such as schools, libraries, and other public access venues, are particularly well situated for use by groups who lack access at home or at work.[9] This factor, plus declining prices of computers, interest at all levels of governments, and the energy and eternal buoyancy of Americans, gives one confidence, or should I weasel with the hackneyed oxymoron "cautious optimism?" In the meanwhile, Census Bureau data seem to indicate that the "gap" is more chasm than crevice; and one can only hope that the next NTIA survey will produce less disheartening statistics. Still, reports like this should not give the impression that the goal of universal computer access is in and of itself a panacea. There are other variables, many of them crucial, in the attempt to bring about a more perfect union wherein no information poor dwell. Heredity, nutrition, peer pressure, family values (yes, the words do have meaning in a post-Quayle era), the environments in which learning takes place, and intangible effects play their roles. Neither a Cassandra nor a Pollyanna be.

TO THE FAMOUS BELONG THE DOMAIN NAMES

We shall not cease from exploration
And the end of all our exploring
Will be to arrive where we started . . .

–T. S. Eliot, *Little Gidding*

On September 10, 1999, NTIA issued a press release announcing that the Department of Commerce, Network Solutions, Inc. (NSI), and the Internet Corporation for Assigned Names and Numbers (ICANN) were about to reach an agreement concerning the management of the domain name system, an operation that has been fraught with vexing problems virtually since its inception. The mechanism for a solution to the difficulties encountered consists of a Shared Registration System, which in its "testbed period" allows multiple licensed accredited registrars to provide name registration services in the .com, .net, and .org domains. The system was developed by NSI pursuant to a "Cooperative Agreement" with the federal government. Presently, ICANN, a California-based, non profit corporation with worldwide representation, is responsible for the accreditation of registrars in the three top level domains noted above. The corporation was created by the Internet community to undertake management of the unruly and ragged domain name system.[10]

The standard categories under the rubric of "intellectual property" have included trade secrets, patents, trademarks, and copyright; but it can be argued that domain names form a legitimate fifth category. They are not the same as trademarks, although second level domain names have been registered as trademarks or service marks. For example, *priceline*.com Inc., a company which has patented business methods (U.S. Patent Number 5,897,620, April 27, 1999) and has been granted a service mark under the heading TRAVEL *PRICELINE* (Filing Date 12/27/96), is making megabucks by dreaming up new tech-driven schemes, patenting them, and spinning them off into businesses.[11] Moreover, although it may be possible to copyright domain names, they do not seem an appropriate subject for copyright law. By definition, they can't be trade secrets. However, the registration of domain names rubs up against trademark law and practice, and therein lies the gravamen of this brief exposition.

The Federal Trade Dilution Act

The Federal Trademark Dilution Act (FTDA) of 1995, codified at 15 U.S.C. §1125 et seq., was signed into law on January 16, 1996. The statute defines the term "dilution" to mean "the lessening of the capacity of a famous mark to identify and distinguish goods or services, regardless of the presence or absence of (1) competition between the owner of the famous mark and other parties, or (2) likelihood of confusion, mistake or deception" (15 U.S.C. § 1127). Section 1125 instructs the courts to deny commercial use of a competing mark or trade name if such use "begins after the mark has become famous and causes dilution of the distinctive quality of the mark. . . . " Exceptions include fair use in competitive advertising (Your Product X takes an hour to sooth a turbulent tummy whereas my Product Y offers relief in a nanosecond); noncommercial use of a mark, "such as parody, satire, and other forms of expression that are not part of a commercial transaction," and "all forms of news reporting and news commentary."[12]

In addition ambiguities in the statute regarding the precise meaning of key words such as "mark" and "famous," the legislative history of the Act (House Report 374, 104th Congress, 1st Session) does little to explicate the meaning of the statute. When a law is ambiguous and plaintiffs challenge one or more of its provisions, the courts in effect become quasi-legislative bodies; and the statute gains clarification only by individual court decisions. But different jurisdictions at the federal appellate level may assign different meanings to the equivocal language, especially if resort to legislative history proves inconclusive. The United States Supreme Court can, of course, resolve the appellate differences; but it may take years for the High Court to call up for review a case or combination of cases that remains unresolved by the lower courts, and the review process usually proceeds at a tardigrade pace.

The first step in acquiring a domain name is the same as that of conducting a patent or trademark search, only much easier. Registrants must check to see if the desired name is already taken. If not, anyone can purchase a domain name by filling out the appropriate forms and paying (as of late 1999) (1) $59 to cover the cost of registration and DNS services by Domain NAmereserve for the first year, and $28 per year thereafter; and (2) a standard $70 fee, which is good for two years, and $35 per year thereafter. The who, what, where, when, and how of domain naming are found at http://d-na.com/faq, including the "Whois," a searchable database to establish if the name you have created is available for registration.

The problems may come after the registrants "own" their domain names. Most domain names are used as symbolic assets of commerce, just as trade names are, whether the latter is a registered mark or is simply recognized as such in common law. The Dilution Act defines "use in commerce" to indicate bona fide use of a mark in the ordinary course of trade and which may legally be regulated by Congress. Moreover, the Lanham Act (15 U.S.C. § 1051 et seq.) governing trademarks, based on the commerce clause of the Constitution (Art. I, sec. 8, cl. 3), "confers broad jurisdictional powers on the courts of the United States" according to a 1952 Supreme Court ruling.[13] But while domain names are mainly used in e-commerce, arguably the fastest growing component of the business world, Congress does not yet regulate that segment of the Internet, popular sentiment being overwhelmingly in favor of laissez faire wheeling and dealing. Notwithstanding, the fact that there have been domain name cases brought under the provisions of the FTDA demonstrates that the courts regard domain names in the same category as trademarks.

David and Goliath

In most cases where the Federal Trademark Dilution Act has been used as a cause of action, the little guy loses, often without a proceeding on the merits, because the small company cannot afford the expense of the legal battle. A hypothetical example: You're prexy of a small company called *Acme* that sells *widgets* in two or three small, contiguous states. You applied for and were granted a domain name in, say, 1994: acme.com. In 1995, a huge corporation named *ACME*, which sells *gadgets* worldwide and has done so for generations, decides that getting a domain name is something that will enhance its already robust business prospects. Imagine the surprise and dismay when big ACME discovers its domain name is "taken" by little Acme. The bigwigs of big ACME are frustrated. They believe that they should command domain because, after all, they are bigger; and in elementary school, the bully always beat up on the smaller kids. Moreover, ACME has been a registered *trademark* lo these many years. So big ACME sues little Acme citing FTDA. The courts have generally sided with the big guys; that is, owners of "famous" marks also get the Internet addresses so that the ACMEs of this world can continue to display their distinctive symbol for all to admire and purchase, even though no one is likely to confuse a widget made in Rhode Island with a gadget sold from Boston to Beijing.

Robin Hood in Reverse

According to Anthony J. DeGidio, Jr., an attorney who has researched this problem in depth, the FTDA "is the antithesis of Robin Hood. It takes from the poor and gives to the rich. Resolution of disputes to date [1997] has been completely unfair. Financial disparity between the parties is almost always certain to appear since the statute only applies to 'famous' marks, and it is difficult to imagine the owner of a famous mark who is not wealthy."[14] Indeed, as DeGidio points out, whereas there have been numerous domain name disputes, relatively few *reported* opinions exist where dilution has been alleged. Most are settled out of court, as was the matter of "avon.com." Carnetta Wong Associates, a small entrepreneur, first registered this domain name, but when the officials of big Avon, the global merchant of cosmetics, toiletries, jewelry, glassware, personal care products, clothing, home decorative products, gifts, etc., discovered its name had been already appropriated, they brought suit against Wong alleging unfair competition, trademark infringement, trademark dilution, and deceptive acts and practices. Avon's case is believed to be the first suit brought under the FTDA. Avon got Wong to relinquish the "avon. com" domain name in an out-of-court settlement.[15] We don't know the terms of the agreement, but other settlements have typically involved money, sometimes scads of it, exchanging hands.

Politicians and Cybersquatters

Money, in fact, is just about the only reprisal available to the little guy. Some ingenious individuals or companies have anticipated the use of domain names that candidates for public office might like to have and registered such juicy political names as gwbush.com, hillaryNo. com, AlBore.com, and others. In the fall of 1998, Zack Exley, a 29-year-old computer programmer in Boston, paid the modest fees for the gwbush.com domain name, and with malice aforethought mounted a Web site as a parody of the Texas governor, "including a fake picture of the candidate snorting coke." Exley, with grand chutzpa, then offered to sell the Bush committee the site for $350,000, an offer that was angrily refused. However, the Bush camp did purchase some 60 domain names, "including Bushsuckz.com, Bushbites.com and Bushblows. com, to keep them out of the hands of pranksters. Those addresses now link users directly to Bush's real site," (http://www. georgewbush.com) but the mischief makers outnumber the politicians and this behavior has become, ho hum, just another aspect of e-commerce.[16]

Hillary and Rudy

In July 1999, first lady Hillary Rodham Clinton formally announced her intention to explore a possible U.S. Senate campaign. But when members of her exploratory committee decided on an appealing

URL, www.hillary2000.org, they discovered it was owned by two San Jose, California, entrepreneurs, who in 1998 had acquired the address. "We thought it was the only name Hillary Clinton would have used in a possible run for the Senate," said one of the owners. "It was a good foresight, and we were really surprised that the name was still available." Hillary's committee ended up paying $6,000 to the owners to gain exclusive rights to the address.[17]

On the other hand, an Internet address, www.HillaryNo.com, was registered by the Friends of Rudolph Giuliani, the first lady's putative rival for the Senate seat vacated by New York Democrat Daniel Patrick Moynihan. According to Rebecca Donatelli, director of the company that manages the site, HillaryNo is "done with humor and it's really more a comparison site than an 'against' site." Still, millions of users have visited the site and thousands have "applied to volunteer for Giuliani's campaign." Being on the Web is "vitally important" for politicians. "If a candidate is not on the Web, or is not using it properly, he's just behind the times," Donatelli says. "The Internet is becoming a cross-generation political tool."[18] One might add that these entrepreneurial shenanigans have also introduced into the language provocative terms like *cybersquatting* and *cyberguerrilla*. It is, in its inimitable way, an example of the revenge of the nerds.

Circumventing the Problem

Parodic oneupmanship does not fall under the province of the Federal Trademark Dilution Law. Moreover, despite the inadequacies of the FTDA, the behemoths do not always prevail in the courts. In October 1999, the Supreme Court declined to hear an appeal by Ringling Brothers and Barnum & Bailey Circus to clarify the scope of the FTDA. Without comment, the justices let stand a lower court ruling that Utah's winter-sports motto "The Greatest Snow on Earth" does not unfairly dilute the circus's familiar, decades-old slogan "The Greatest Show on Earth."[19] This, of course, is a trademark case, but the distinction between trademarks and domain names under current law is tenuous.

The problem of domain names purchased by a savvy individual or institution to preempt the names established companies are known by may be amenable to resolution without litigation. As Steven Levy of *Newsweek* remarks,

> Some companies are already working on directory systems, in portals or browsers, that bypass domain names and use other

means to link people with the sites they seek. Leading the pack is a technology called Real Names, which has deals to be embedded in the searching and browsing technology of big players like AltaVista, Inktomi and Microsoft. . . . If such directory services become ubiquitous, "the obsession with domain names will go away," says Esther Dyson, chairman (sic) of ICANN, the non-profit organization charged with resolving Internet-addressing issues. "They'll still be there, but people won't always need them to go directly where they want to on the Web."[20]

WIPO and Cybersquatting

Well, maybe. Trademark registration is managed by a federal agency, the United States Patent and Trademark Office. Domain names are not under U.S. government control. The World Intellectual Property Organization (WIPO), a specialized international intergovernmental body, published a report in April 1999 recommending techniques to protect trademark rights online, including preferred procedures for domain name registrars, dispute resolution guidelines, and exclusions for famous trademarks. It also recommended that administrative dispute policies be adopted for combating bad faith registration of domain names that violate trademark rights, a euphemism for cybersquatting.

The trouble with this *Final Report of the WIPO Internet Domain Name Process* is that it lacks consensus among the parties that have engaged in its creation. For example, A. Michael Froomkin, professor of law at the University of Miami School of Law who served on the panel of experts that advised WIPO on the report, stated that the guidelines on how to protect famous or well-known marks use "vague and prejudicial criteria." Froomkin and others advocated "including a cap on the number of marks that could be certified as famous . . . under the proposal." Don Heath, president of the Internet Society, "agreed that the report would be better if it included an upper limit on the number of famous marks." Heath also said that "the definition of what would be considered a famous mark needed improvement as well." WIPO argued that "such a quota would be arbitrary and unworkable."[21] Perhaps we need a multilateral treaty. Right now, though, it sounds to me like deja vu all over again.

A REFERENCE QUICKIE

Q. What's the real name of a personage in politics whose statements are, well, impolitic?

A. Follow this search strategy: (1) Visit the federal trademark office URL, <http://trademarks.uspto.gov>; (2) Type in Serial Number 75-460259.

ENDNOTES

1. Berra, the former catcher for the New York Yankees, is credited in the 15th edition of *Bartlett's Familiar Quotations* with the immortal phrase "The game isn't over till it's over."

2. *Falling Through the Net: Introduction* (http://www.ntia.doc.gov/ntiahome/fttn99/introduction.html).

3. *Falling Through the Net: Executive Summary* (http://www.ntia.doc.gov/ntiahome/fttn99/execsummary. html).

4. Ibid.

5. Jonathan Alter, "Bridging the Digital Divide," *Newsweek*, September 20, 1999, p. 55.

6. Ibid.

7. "Technology: Creating a New Generation of Haves and Have-Nots?" *Reputation Management* (http://www.prcentral.com).

8. The Equity and Technology Discussion Group, December 2, 1997 (http://www.aace.virginia.edu).

9. Supra, note 3.

10. Department of Commerce Press Release, September 10, 1999 (www.ntia.doc/gov/ntiahome/press).

11. *Newsweek*, September 20, 1999, p. 48.

12. *Congressional Record* (daily edition), December 29, 1995, p. S19310.

13. *United States Steel v. Bulova Watch Company*, 344 U.S. 280, 293 (1952).

14. Anthony J. DeGidio, Jr., "Internet Domain Names and the Federal Trademark Dilution Act: A Law for the Rich and Famous," (http://www.lawoffices.net/tradedom/sempap.htm), screen 20 of 24.

15. Ibid., screen 10 of 24. Other domain name cases noted by DeGidio under FTDA include the newyorker.com, gateway.com, realpages.com, and candyland.com.

16. Martha Brant, "The Mouse that Roars," *Newsweek*, September 20, 1999, p. 53.

17. Giada Zampano, "Hillary Campaigns Online," *PC World*, July 8, 1999 (http://pcworld.com).

18. Ibid.

19. *Findlaw Legal News*, October 5, 1999 (http://dowjones.wsj.com/i/law).

20. Steven Levy, "We're Running Out of Dot.Coms," *Newsweek*, October 11, 1999, p. 79.

21. "WIPO Recommends Procedures to Protect Trademarks Against 'Cyber squatting'," *IP Law Weekly* 1: 1, 11 (May 13, 1999).

Index